Oil on Ice: Alaskan Wilderness at the Crossroads is a Sierra Club *Battlebook*. The first. And maybe the most important. For the story of that wilderness and of the pressures to extract the black gold that lies beneath it is nothing less than what ecologist Barry Commoner has called "a microcosm of the whole environmental issue."

The issue in Alaska is the prospect of an estimated 100 billion barrels of oil buried beneath the frigid landscape of America's last great wilderness. But the issue raises a question: What effect will the extraction of that treasure have on Alaska's fragile environment, particularly if the oil is transported to market through an equally fragile trans-Alaskan pipeline?

oil on ice

Alaskan wilderness
at the crossroads

by Tom Brown

edited,
with an introduction, by
Richard Pollak

Sierra Club   San Francisco • New York

Copyright © 1971 by the Sierra Club.
All rights reserved.
Library of Congress catalog card number: 73-149449
International Standard Book number 87156-046-1
Designed by Charles Curtis, produced by Heliographic, Inc.,
New York, and printed in the United States of America by
The Guinn Company, Inc.

Tom Brown's analysis of the Alaskan oil
situation appeared originally as a series of articles
in the *Anchorage Daily News*. The Sierra Club is grateful
to the *Daily News* for permission to use that material as
the foundation for this book.

Contents

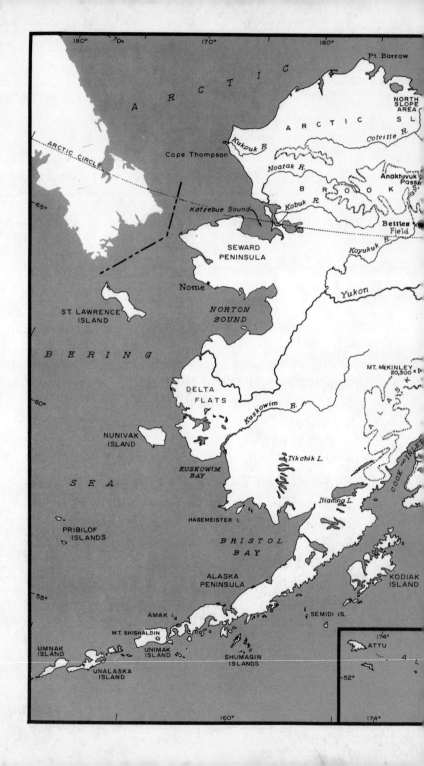

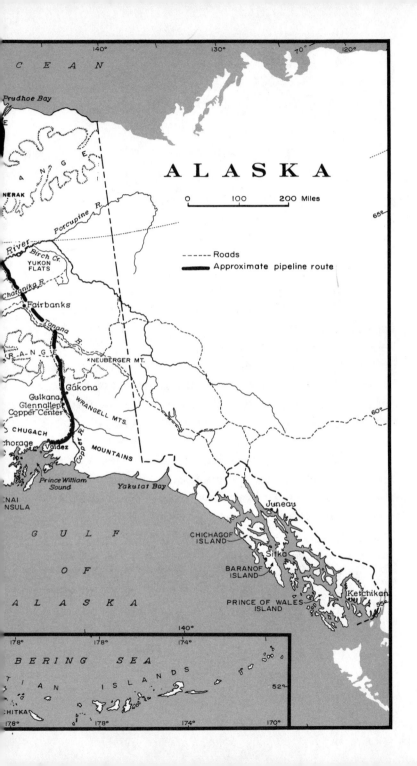

A letter from the Brooks Range:

"As I write this a great caravan of heavily laden trucks is growling over a new winter road which yesterday reached the Eskimo village in Anaktuvuk Pass at the central top of the range. Yesterday wrote the end of Anaktuvuk Pass as it was—a small village of inland Eskimos still dependent upon migrating herds of caribou. It may have written the beginning of the end of the great caribou herds, majestic mountain sheep and the wolf. It was certainly the end of thousands of years of solitude as the great diesel trucks thundered up the John River Valley on their way to the North Slope and the great oil strike near Prudhoe Bay. . . . There is no time left. . . . We must preserve any wilderness area left on this planet that we have now seen from the moon to be our home, or the opportunity is lost forever. Fortunately the Brooks Range is in the State of Alaska in the United States of America, and we can save it now. Next month, tomorrow, will be too late."

Samuel A. Wright
February 15, 1969

Introduction

by Richard Pollak

"Hell, this country's so goddamn big that even if industry ran wild we could never wreck it. We can have our cake and eat it, too."

—Henry Pratt
executive assistant to former
Gov. Keith H. Miller of Alaska

One contemplates Alaska today with a numbing sense of historical perspective. We have seen this pristine land before: the United States at its birth two centuries ago. Now, once again, we are playing out the scenario that has reduced so much of the nation to an environmental theater of the absurd. The cake this time is oil—an estimated 100 billion barrels, maybe more—buried beneath the frigid landscape of our last great wilderness, a stunning national outback the size of Texas, California and Montana combined. To get this newly found black treasure to market, the oil industry seeks to lay down an 800-mile pipeline from the arctic tundra of Alaska's North Slope south to the ice-free port of Valdez. Eventually, two million barrels of hot oil would sluice daily from the throbbing wells in the frozen north to mammoth tankers waiting at the terminus on Prince William Sound.

En route, this viscous crude would travel the breadth of Alaska's most fragile ecosystems: from the ice-worn coast of Prudhoe Bay, across the lichen-sprinkled tundra of the North Slope, up rolling foothills into the glaciated grandeur of the Brooks Range, through barren, snowbound mountain passes, down to the valleys and forests of the interior highlands, hard by the growing population center of Fairbanks, through the Alaska Range, the Copper River Basin and Chugach Mountains and, finally, down to the waiting ships at Valdez. The 48-inch steel pipe would snake through the once-untrammeled habitats of hundreds of thousands of caribou, of wolves and Barren Ground grizzlies, Dall sheep and moose, the peregrine falcon (elsewhere, nearly extinct) and millions of migratory birds and waterfowl. On its way, the oil would cross two dozen rivers (including the Yukon), well over a hundred streams and border scores of lakes in whose sparkling waters salmon, char, pike and myriad other fish abound.

As recently planned, all but 50 miles of the pipeline would be buried four to ten feet underground. Much of this earth is permafrost, the perennially frozen subsoil so vital to the stabilization of the Alaskan environment. Oil coursing through the pipeline at up to 170 degrees F. would thaw the subsoil into a trans-Alaska quagmire, with incalculable consequences. Earthquakes, for example, have a particularly chaotic effect on waterlogged ground, their vibrations turning it to liquid and causing catastrophic slides. The pipeline would pass through three major earthquake zones.

But it would take far less than an earthquake to rupture so long and vulnerable a pipeline, and even oilmen concede that spills are inevitable. What they don't readily admit is that a pipeline break in Alaska would make the *Torrey Canyon* and Santa Barbara disasters seem like so much spilt milk. Although electronic sensors could detect ruptures within microseconds after they occur, closing one of the pipeline's 73 cutoff valves—which are to be 30 feet high and weigh 60,000 pounds—would take several minutes. Even where the pipeline runs level, thousands of gallons would pour out and destroy fish and wildlife for miles around. Where the conduit slopes down from the mountains, the spillage and destruction would be many times worse.

In Alaska, moreover, the intrusion of industrial man has a uniquely severe effect. The state's ecological metabolism falters at the slightest disruption. For example, the U.S. Geological Survey reports, ". . . The simple passage of a tracked vehicle that destroys the vegetation mat is enough to upset the delicate balance and to cause the top of the permafrost layer to thaw. This thawing can cause differential settlement of the surface of the ground, drainage problems, and severe frost action. Once the equilibrium is upset, the whole process can feed on itself and be practically impossible to reverse."

Equally critical, the icy climate keeps matter non-biodegradable—not susceptible to decomposition. As a result, the environment acts as a giant freezer, preserving man's tracks and debris wherever he leaves them. The trail of a wagon driven across the tundra of the Seward Peninsula two times in 1920 remains unhealed a half century later. The tracks made by World War II vehicles on Amchitka Island in the Aleutians look as if they might have been created a week ago. At Amchitka, Point Barrow and the long-abandoned Naval Petroleum Reserve just west of the present oil concession on the North Slope, arctic junkyards of Quonset huts, wrecked planes and cars and just now rusting oil drums stretch for miles in every direction. Now, the 450,-858-acre concession on the North Slope is daily raked and scarred as the oil industry probes its bonanza with all the alien technology it can muster. Testifying to the oilmen's success, the industrial smears stain the gray-white terrain like so many grotesque Rorschach blots. Already, says University of Alaska ecologist Robert B. Weeden, "Oil explorations in northern Alaska have destroyed the wilderness character of an area bigger than the state of Massachusetts."

To the upbeat roll of public relations drums, the oil companies insist they had no idea how delicate the arctic was and now promise to take every precaution in the future. As evidence of these new intentions, the oilmen cite a variety of good works. Humble Oil, for example, flies University of Alaska professors down to the "Lower 48" to brief incoming oil hands on the special nature of the arctic environment. Atlantic Richfield is investigating the possibility of using plastic to insulate the permafrost so the industry will need to scoop up less gravel from rivers and streams in constructing roads, drilling pads and the pipeline. And several of the 15 major oil companies now drilling on the North Slope have not only tidied up their housekeeping but hauled away some of the litter they found when they arrived. These and other precautions—like aerial surveillance of the pipeline (if it comes to that)—will all doubtless prove useful. In some instances, they may even flow from a genuine sense of corporate responsibility. But in the end precautionary mitigation of the oil industry's overall impact on Alaska will be marginal at best. No matter how many points the industry accrues for neatness, the hard fact remains that in pumping out two million barrels of oil a day industry will irrevocably hash up the North Slope with a maze of roads, feeder pipes and drill sites. And whatever the safeguards, an 800-mile pipeline is certain to burst periodically once the daily dose of hot petroleum starts squirting down to Valdez.

Two million barrels a day would be just the beginning, for once the pipeline was built, the industry's march through the rest of Alaska could become irreversible. The North Slope is but one of 10 sedimentary basins in the state that hold promise—or, in the case of Cook Inlet, proof—that huge deposits of oil lie below the soil. In fact, as much as half of Alaska's land mass and vast offshore shelf is underlain with geological formations that tantalize the oil companies. Just east of the eager drillers on the North Slope, for example, lies the Arctic National Wildlife Range, an 8.9-million-acre refuge that provides a critical calving ground for thousands of caribou cows. Beneath the range, it is believed, more oil awaits the takers, who even now reportedly are conducting clandestine seismic explorations in the area.

How the taking of all this oil will ravage the Alaskan landscape is not simply a matter of hand-wringing speculation. The proof of the gummy, black pudding can be found every day on the waters of Cook Inlet and on the Kenai Peninsula. In this region, due west of Valdez, the oil companies made their first big Alaskan strike in the summer of 1957. In exchange for the right to set up their rigs in the Kenai National Moose Range, the firms vowed to protect the character of the range and its horned inhabitants as well. And under the strict supervision of the U.S. Department of the Interior, the oilmen established what many regard as a model oil field. Still, a survey by the U.S. Fish and Wildlife Service found that despite this "high degree of co-operation, long-term scarring effects to the environment, the disturbance of all wildlife, pollution dangers to fisheries and waterfowl waters, increased fire hazards and human occupancy foreign to a natural habitat have resulted in serious detriment to the range's objectives, invalidating earlier thoughts to the contrary." Despite this warning—made in 1964 —more and more rigs have sprouted on the peninsula. And though oilmen in the moose range continue to police the area, their counterparts in some other fields are not nearly so fastidious. Out from under the watchful eyes of federal inspectors, they have heedlessly torn up the landscape, scattered industrial waste at will and made oil spills a recurring event in Cook Inlet.

During a two-year period that ended in the spring of 1968, almost 100 oil pollution incidents were recorded in the huge bay. When a drilling platform first taps a well, for example, more than 100 barrels of crude are often simply pumped into the water until the oil starts running pure and the well is capped. Added to this, of course, is the inevitable spillage from the growing number of tankers in the inlet. In the winter of 1967, after a tanker ruptured a compartment while docking, 63,-000 gallons of oil poured into the water and spread for miles. Two months later, the 29,000-ton *Rebecca* emptied thousands of barrels of oily ballast into the inlet before berthing to take on a holdful of Kenai crude. Such willful pollution has long been routine tanker practice, playing no small part in what French oceanographer Jacques-Yves Cousteau regards as the cause of death of 40 percent of the world's sea life. Following the *Rebecca* incident, Alaskan officials adopted harsh penalties for ballast dumping, even threatening to confiscate offending tankers. And in late 1970, Secretary of Transportation John A. Volpe called for an international agreement that would end the time-honored dumping tradition by 1975. Enforcing such a regulation would be difficult at best in the Gulf of Alaska alone. Even if every quart of ballast were treated ashore—as the oil companies now promise—the water returned to the inlet would still be distinctly foreign to the delicate estuaries on the inlet's edge. In addition, strictures against platform leaks and spills from both underwater pipelines and shore facilities remain woefully weak.

The impact of this pollution—past, present and potential—is as clear as the sea is not. Water may roll off a duck's back, but oil doesn't. To date, thousands of waterfowl have lost the slimy battle of Cook Inlet; and even if the industry were to add new safeguards, thousands more will die, along with king crab, salmon and, unless the spillage ends, the entire biota of the inlet. And given the vastly greater quantity of oil the industry seeks to pump into Valdez, the implications for Prince William Sound are infinitely worse. Should an earthquake and tidal wave shatter the region—as they did in 1964—this time the stakes would include perhaps a dozen tankers in the harbor and as much as 20 million barrels of crude in the storage tanks of the pipeline's terminus. A fraction of that oil would turn the sound into another Lake Erie and seal a slick lid over the Gulf of Alaska's multimillion-dollar fishing industry for years to come.

Nor would the pollution threat diminish if the industry opted to bring its newfound oil to market directly from the North Slope in ships like the S. S. *Manhattan,* the 115,000-ton dead-weight tanker that plowed through the icy Northwest Passage in 1969. On the contrary, oil congeals at frigid temperatures, and a single spill could visit incalculable mischief on the arctic ecosystem. If 30 or more tankers began crashing through the treacherous passage, the effect of their pollution, in fact, could easily become global. In determining the world's weather, no single land mass plays a more critical role than the arctic ice pack. Once widespread, oil pollution from the fleet of tankers and from the North Slope field as well could seriously alter arctic heat patterns, upsetting fundamental weather balances thousands of miles away.

Alaska, then, is nothing less than what ecologist Barry Commoner so aptly calls "a living microcosm of the whole environmental issue." A microcosm, moreover, that covers some 586,000 square miles, stretches 3,200 miles through four time zones from the tip of the Aleutians to Prince Rupert on the border of British Coumbia, whose 33,000 miles of coastline are half again that of the rest of the nation's seaboard and whose awesome precincts offer Americans their last chance to preserve, in Dr. Weeden's words, "an embodiment of the frontier mythology, the sense of horizons unexplored, the mystery of uninhabited miles." Of the 2.3 billion acres of land and water in the 50 states, only about

10 percent remains truly unspoiled. Almost all of
this wilderness is in Alaska.

It took two centuries to desecrate the 48 states.
Given the impact of modern technology, the population boom and the ever-shrinking supply of open
space elsewhere, it should take only a decade or two
to foul Alaska. "The discovery of oil," warns Dr.
Weeden, "has telescoped the margin of time for
wilderness preservation into a very few years. . . .
there is no other private industry with similar ability to amass huge amounts of capital, and move men
and equipment to remote parts of the earth [and]
there is no other industry that changes the appearance of the landscape over such large areas in the
process of looking for a resource."

To justify this rape, the oil companies and their
supporters flay us with conventional wisdom. They
argue, for example, that Alaska desperately needs
the industry because it is a "poor" state. And in the
one-dimensional context of the cash nexus, so it
seems. Long little more than a colony dependent on
Washington for more than $1 of every $2 spent
within its borders, Alaska suffers the nation's
highest unemployment rate and its native Aleuts,
Eskimos and Indians (one-fifth the total state population of 304,000) are likely the poorest citizens in
the United States.

Anticipating fat profits, the industry has already
invested upward of $2 billion in the North Slope
and the pipeline and is prepared to spend a billion
or so more before a single drop of arctic oil starts

moving to market. At capacity, the pipeline would generate $200 million a year for Alaska in royalties and severance taxes. And this would come on top of the $900 million the industry paid the state in September, 1969, simply for the privilege of drilling on the North Slope. Predictably, all these fast bucks have given most Alaskans an acute case of Klondike fever, complete with gilded fantasies of transforming the state—in the words of one former resident—"from a frozen Appalachia to a frozen Kuwait." This prospecter mentality, of course, smogged the air, curdled the waters and blighted the cities of the rest of the nation. Excusing it here on the ground that Alaska is poor is like telling an Eskimo he can have a refrigerator if he will allow oil drills to obliterate his hunting grounds. Yet in no real sense is Alaska poor at all. On the contrary, it is rich not only in that rarest of resources— wilderness—but in the opportunities wilderness provides to develop such industries as fishing and tourism. Properly managed, these would impinge on the sensitive Alaskan environment infinitely less than would the extraction of oil, and at the same time provide a firm economic foundation for a population unlikely to exceed half a million by the end of the century. As for the state's 57,000 natives, they live in squalid villages not because funds are lacking to help them but because, like all dark-skinned Americans in our history, they have been systematically exploited and mistreated. Only now is Washington finally dealing with their long-standing claims to ancestral lands taken by Alaska's white settlers in time-honored exchange for fast talk, cheap liquor and the ravages of tuberculosis and syphilis. But while the natives wait for Congress to translate this tardy justice into acres and dollars, Alaska's power brokers seem in no hurry to provide even interim assistance. The natives continue to subsist in abject poverty throughout the state while the $900 million in oil lease money sits in banks gathering nearly $200,000 in interest a day. And the state legislature can't decide what to do with it.

When jackpot psychology fails to persuade their opponents, the industry offers up perhaps its most specious argument of all—that the North Slope oil is desperately needed to head off an acute fuel shortage in the heavily populated areas of the U. S. And, indeed, so it seemed in the early fall of 1970 as scare headlines warned that thousands of citizens faced a chilly winter for lack of residual crude to heat their homes and apartments. Yet the fact of the matter is that no real shortage existed then, exists now, or appears at all likely in the near future. As The New York Times correctly noted early on: "If there ever was a man-made crisis, this is it."

The threads of this manufactured emergency are admittedly complex, a tangle that includes the volatile politics of the Middle East, the demand for cleaner fuel in the U.S., a temporary shortage of tankers, stringent restrictions on imports, a vague energy policy set by a score of Federal agencies and, not the least, the organized obfuscation of the oil industry. Despite this confusion, two things have long been clear: the nation could quickly end its fuel "crisis" if (1) domestic oil production were not rigged low to keep the price stable and (2) imports were not rigidly discouraged. When President Nixon belatedly accepted these facts in December, 1970, the Great Oil Shortage became the economic non-event of the year. By authorizing an increase in the production from offshore wells and letting in additional Canadian oil, the President in one stroke added up 500,000 barrels a day to the U.S. supply.

Beyond this immediate relief, the U.S. and Canada are now busily working out a continental energy policy that would provide, in the words of a joint communique issued by the two governments late in 1970, "full and unimpeded access to United States markets of Canadian crude oil and petroleum products, surplus to Canadian commercial and security requirements." In 1971, the agreement is expected to add 100,000 barrels to the 750,000 Canada already exports daily to the U.S. And, given Canada's vast oil reserves and relatively small population (21 million), its exportable surplus will likely grow markedly in the next decade. These exports, along with existing reserves and the enormous amounts of untapped shale oil in the U.S., leave the nation nowhere near the precarious position so dear to the oil company propagandists. (Significantly, too, the industry-generated flap over shortages turned entirely on heating oil; not once was it suggested that motor fuel might become scarce, a fact that reflects the industry's devotion to that highly profitable product and the super-polluter it feeds, the internal combustion engine.)

In light of the ephemeral nature of the energy shortfall, there appears no immediate justification whatsoever to violate further the North Slope, much less construct an 800-mile pipeline from Prudhoe Bay to Prince William Sound. And the long view proves even less persuasive. Despite all the superlatives employed to describe the black pool beneath the North Slope, the crude there would satisfy no more than five per cent of the U.S. demand once it began flowing to market through the pipeline. True, that percentage could be increased, but only by gradually pocking the rest of Alaska with oil wells and crisscrossing the landscape with more and more pipelines. Predictably, the oil industry vigorously denies such expansionist aims—all the while poking around in the wilderness for other fields to tap.

Alaska may contribute only a small percentage to the U.S. oil supply, but some other percentages are more impressive. As Alaskan economist Arlon R. Tussing explained at a Department of Interior hearing not long ago, "The anticipated rate of return to (oil companies working the Slope) would be 43 percent." Even should the cost of the pipeline double, Tussing maintained, the returns would still approach 36 percent. These huge potential profits are made possible by an Oil Import Quota Program that severely limits domestic consumption of cheap foreign oil, artificially inflates the price of U.S. crude and, by conservative estimates, costs the American consumer some $7 billion a year. Historically, Congress has justified this protectionist policy on the grounds that national security requires that the U.S. not become too dependent on foreign oil. But as Sen. Philip A. Hart has pointed out, "The prime effect of such 'security' measures has been to insulate the American market from the low world prices for oil and petroleum products."

The planned plunder of Alaska's North Slope seems particularly criminal at a time when the government could begin to develop other energy sources —sources calculated to reduce the nation's dependency on a fuel that has become its worst pollutant. Beyond nuclear energy, scientists now are experimenting with myriad new power possibilities, among them: superconductivity, the transmission of electricity through hyper-cooled conduits without resistance or loss; magnetohydrodynamics, the generation of electricity from a supersonic flow of hot ionized gases, and solar energy, the conversion of sunlight to electricity by synergizing electronic and space technology. Much research remains, of course, and new environmental problems (such as thermal pollution from atomic plants) will doubtless arise. But with the intelligent reordering of fiscal and scientific priorities, a viable, efficient, inexpensive and cleaner alternative to oil should not be far off. If we can get to the moon, etc.

Not surprisingly, President Nixon is marching in the opposite direction. To help determine the nation's long range energy requirements, the Administration has asked for a "high-level" study from the

National Petroleum Council. The National Petroleum Council is not an organization of bakers. As
for the immediate issue of the trans-Alaska pipeline, every indication pointed to its approval early
in 1971. Whatever the President's reasons for firing
Secretary of Interior Walter J. Hickel, disagreement
over bringing out Alaska's oil was not among them.
"There was no conflict with the President," says
Patrick P. Ryan, Hickel's principal aide and one of
the six Interior officials dismissed along with the
secretary. "Both agreed that the pipeline should be
built once the consortium meets the Federal standards." And in the words of John Horton, a special
assistant in the secretary's office who has shepherded
the pipeline permit request through Interior, "those
standards are designed so the companies will be able
to meet them." Hickel's successor, Secretary of the
Interior Rogers C. B. Morton, a noted Nixon team
player, is unlikely to break step with this plan.

In the following pages, Tom Brown, a knowledgeable reporter for the *Anchorage Daily News,* ex-
amines the Alaska oil boom and its many ramifica-
tions in considerable detail. He brings to his task
neither the polemics of the conservationist nor the
puffery of the oil industry flack. He brings instead
an objective, clear-headed analysis of what oil on
ice means for Alaska. Brown leaves conclusions to
the reader. Without reservation, the Sierra Club
feels the evidence warrants only one conclusion:

The oil companies should dismantle their rigs
and go home.

1. Discovery:

Flare-out at Prudhoe One

As winter descended on Alaska's North Slope after
the short, bright summer of 1967, the oilmen set up
their outpost at an inhospitable place called
Prudhoe Bay. Inland, then, vast herds of caribou
began their seasonal migration, moving across the
tundra in a living tide. The Barren Ground grizzlies put on their last fat before hibernating. Millions of waterfowl winged south. But the oilmen
settled in. After freeze-up, when the tundra was
rock-hard and could support the weight, they erect-
ed their drilling rig at a site carefully chosen by oil
company geologists. And as the long arctic night
advanced, they drilled. They drilled throughout the
dark winter months, through bitter cold and blind-
ing whiteouts. They drilled until they found what
they were looking for 9,000 feet beneath America's
last great wilderness.

First word of the strike came in January, 1968, when the Atlantic Richfield Co. (ARCO) announced that its well, named Prudhoe Bay State No. 1 and drilled on lease acreage held jointly with the Humble Oil and Refining Co., had flared "a substantial flow of gas" at 8,500 feet. Drilling proceeded amid growing industry optimism and, a month later, ARCO reported it had cased in the well at 8,708 feet through a 470-foot sand body, the lower 70 feet of which was "believed oil-saturated on the basis of core examination."

Early that March, ARCO disclosed it would drill a second well, to be called Sag River State No. 1 (after the nearby Sagavanirktok River), about seven miles southeast of the discovery well in the same geological formation. This was generally interpreted as certain evidence that the company had what it thought was a major find, and confirmation came a week later when ARCO indicated that the Prudhoe Bay well had flowed oil at the rate of 1,152 barrels a day in initial tests. The drilling rig was hastily moved across country to the new location and soon was churning into the earth again. And on June 25, ARCO announced that the Sag River well had supported the Prudhoe Bay find, having "encountered oil in the same Triassic formation." Robert O. Anderson, ARCO's board chairman, cautiously conceded the discovery was "significant," but insisted that the true dimensions of the find could only be determined by further testing and exploratory drilling. DeGolyer and MacNaughton,

leading oil consultants from Dallas, were more san-
guine. "In our opinion," they announced soon after
ARCO's second strike, "this important discovery
could develop into a field with recoverable reserves
of some five to ten billion barrels of oil, which
would rate as one of the largest petroleum accumu-
lations known to the world today."

Though the ARCO payoff was a long time coming, few knowledgeable oilmen were greatly sur-
prised. The Alaskan arctic, after all, had long been
considered a highly promising area for oil prospecting. Early explorers reported numerous surface oil
seeps on the North Slope, and the Eskimos had
observed them for centuries. Long ago, geologists
discovered a series of classic anticlines—the dome-
like rock formations that often serve as oil traps—
beneath the tundra of the Slope. In the 1940s and
1950s, the U.S. Navy drilled 37 exploratory wells
and 45 core tests on Naval Petroleum Reserve No.
4, a vast area of the Slope due west of the Prudhoe
field. But, in terms of a commercial find, that effort
proved fruitless. After the navy suspended the operation in 1952, public interest in the Slope flagged,
and the dream of mining black gold there was
largely forgotten by most Alaskans.

But not by the oil companies. Despite the extraordinary cost of artic oil exploration, their interest in the Slope remained lively. Surface geology
and seismic sounding parties roamed the tundra in
the 1950s and 1960s and eight wildcat wells were
drilled, six by British Petroleum and Sinclair and

one each by Colorado Oil and Gas and Union Oil. The discovery role played by ARCO, in fact, was largely a matter of luck. In 1966, the firm decided to drill a wildcat well on North Slope leases it had acquired in a state lease sale. Two locations were proposed, one at Prudhoe Bay and another further inland near the Sagavanirktok River. ARCO opted for the latter, called it Susie Unit No. 1 and poured $4.5 million into it before abandoning it as dry. The company decided to try one more time before giving up on the Slope and set up its rig at Prudhoe Bay State No. 1. This time the oil spouted—into the Great Alaska Oil Rush.

Between mid-1968 and mid-1969, every major company with lease holdings on the Slope rushed to explore them. The number of wells increased from two to more than 30. Companies without actual lease holdings sent seismic crews to find prime unleased land in preparation for the state's impending sale of new leases on the Slope. On the cool, gray morning of September 10, 1969, dozens of oilmen and their bankers lined up inside the Sydney Laurence Auditorium in downtown Anchorage, clutching briefcases packed with several hundred million dollars. Quietly they filed up and presented state officials with sealed envelopes containing bid checks for 179 tracts of land totaling some 450,000 acres. For the next several hours the bids were read off, tract by tract. And by the end of the day, Alaska had collected $900 million for its oil and gas concessions in the richest lease sale in history. At

the height of activity, 2,500 oilmen were laboring
on the Slope, and the industry's investment had
soared to $2 billion as it prepared to construct an
800-mile pipeline across the width of the state to
get its new find to market.

While the oil companies scrambled to get operational on the Slope, most Alaskans watched with
bemused wonderment. It took a long time for the
importance of what was happening to sink in. Even
during the contentious 1969 session of the state
legislature, then Gov. Keith H. Miller had refused
to raise the official estimate that the state would
receive only $11 million from the September oil
lease sale because that was all it had gotten from
similar sales in the past. To do otherwise, the governor said, would be "irresponsible." Thornton F.
Bradshaw, president of Atlantic Richfield, meanwhile, said he believed the state would realize a
minimum of $1 billion from the sale. Other oilmen
privately predicted the total would be in the $1.3
billion-$1.5 billion range. However, that was before
Thomas E. Kelly, the state's commissioner of natural resources, announced that the state would sell
only about one-third of its 1.2 million acres of
North Slope land.

The $900 million Alaska did get was a mind-
boggling sum for a state whose budget for the
1969-70 fiscal year totaled less than $154 million;
whose economy for years had been dependent on
federal agencies for six of every ten dollars spent
within its borders; whose first inhabitants, the Eski-

mos, Indians and Aleuts (referred to collectively as natives), now constitute 20 percent of the population and live for the most part in abject poverty, and that urgently needs the most basic social facilities, including schools, hospitals, roads, sewers and even pure drinking water (in a state thas has 40 percent of the nation's total supply of fresh water). And the initial income from the lease sale would be only the beginning. Through production royalties and severance taxes, the state will receive about one-fifth the value of the oil after production and transportation costs have been deducted—potentially $4.5 billion to $6 billion over the 15 to 30-year life of the field (conservatively rated at 15 billion barrels).

The pool of oil beneath the North Slope, which some now predict may eventually yield more than 100 billion barrels, has triggered Alaska's first major environmental crisis, pitting the dynamics of development against the conservation of natural values and placing two of the state's most valuable resources—oil and wilderness—in direct conflict. A resolution of that conflict still is not in sight. On the one hand—oil. The income from it could help transform Alaska from a pauper state into one of the wealthiest; it could turn enormous profits for a number of oil companies, which play a major role in the national economy; and, on a larger scale, it could allow the United States to prevent the widening of the gap between the amount of oil it produces and the amount it uses, a development with important implications for the nation's foreign policy. On the other hand—wilderness. It is scarcer already than oil and in the long run (even a few oilmen agree) it almost certainly will prove more valuable. Alaska is America's last big piece of it, and the North Slope and the majestic Brooks Range to the south make up a considerable part of what wilderness Alaska has left.

Is it technically possible to remove the oil without ruining the wilderness? If not, how much damage can be considered acceptable? If the tundra is damaged now, can it be repaired? What effects will oil development have on the wildfowl, the grizzlies, the caribou and the wolves on land, the fish in the streams, and the seals, walrus, whales and polar bears offshore? What is the oil industry's responsibility? What is the public's responsibility? And behind these questions lies the singular reminder of Dr. Robert Weeden, assistant professor of game management at the University of Alaska and a leading conservationist: "America has only one arctic. It's in Alaska and north of the Brooks Range. It seems to me we should be taking pretty good care of it."

2. The Land:

Sparkling tundra, whistling crags

Before the ARCO strike in the winter of 1968, few
people outside Alaska had ever heard of either the
North Slope or the Brooks Range. Even within the
state, not many knew much about them. But as the
importance of the oil find and its likely impact on
America's vanishing wilderness became clear, some
people learned quickly. They learned that the
North Slope rolls down from the peaks of the
Brooks Range for a distance that varies from 40 to
150 miles until it reaches the arctic coast on the
Beaufort Sea. Near the foothills, it is a rolling,
hummocky land, scoured by rivers and streams,
well drained and dry in the summer. In the north,
the hills become smaller and finally trail off altogether. The rivers and streams lose grade, flowing
in serpentine coils toward the sea, where they fan

into broad, gravelly deltas. Along the coast, and for miles inland, the terrain is table flat, dappled with thousands of lakes, poorly drained. It was on this plain, not far from the sea, that ARCO made its first strike.

With the exception of a few sheltered valleys in the foothills where scattered stands of trees persist, plant life on the North Slope is limited to a profusion of lichens, dwarf shrubs and scrub conifers that never grow higher than a few inches. In the summer, wildflowers also punctuate the dun tundra. Huge herds of caribou feed on this vegetation—at least 360,000 of them, perhaps three times that number. There are the Porcupine Herd and the Arctic Herd, the latter roaming the general area from Prudhoe Bay to the west, migrating through mountain passes to the South Slope for the winter, then following the retreating snow north in the spring. The Porcupine Herd occupies the Arctic National Wildlife Range just east of Prudhoe Bay, and regularly crosses the border into Canada on its seasonal migrations. The caribou shares its North Slope habitat with a variety of other species, among them the rare Barren Ground grizzly, a curious, often unpredictable bear generally somewhat smaller than its cousins further south; wolves that range in color from white to coal black, wolverines, arctic foxes and occasional polar bears. The lakes along the arctic littoral are critical way stations for migratory waterfowl. Millions of these birds nest and breed their young in Canada's Yukon and Northwest Ter-

ritories, move over to the North Slope to molt in
the lakes, then fly south for the winter.

Winter is the only genuine season in the high
arctic. It sweeps in with finality in October—
sometimes even earlier—covering the Slope and the
mountains beyond with snow. From a plane, the
only practical means of rapid, long-distance travel
in any season, the Slope glows gray-white in the
thin twilight, appearing faintly rippled like a sea
frozen suddenly in motion. Patches of black ice dot
the landscape where winds have swept away the
snow. The land is flat, monotonously, unrelievedly
flat. And cold. Often 65 degrees below zero, sometimes lower. Perhaps worse for the unacclimated
human, it is night here for months. The sun never
edges above the horizon and day at most is a frigid
pastel hanging in the south. Yet the Slope is almost
never dark in the pitch-black way that some winter
nights can bring in lower latitudes. The snow is
always present, reflecting the twilit southern sky
and the light from the moon and stars. And much
of the time, when the sky is clear, the northern
lights drip over the frozen tundra in a brilliant and
ever-changing display of red and green and gold and
purple.

The Brooks Range to the south is Alaska's spine,
separating the high arctic of the North Slope from
the subarctic interior of the state. This rugged
jumble of spiky spires, smooth humps and triangu-
lar glacial wedges is the largest virgin wilderness in
the U.S. Only some 200 persons inhabit an expanse

the size of Italy. Among the peaks are sheltered valleys, emerald lakes and icy streams quick with white water—a stunning setting as untamed as the wind that whistles through the crags. It is a forbidding land of cold and deep shadows, of snow glittering under the moon and of mountain tops sprayed golden by the sun when it rises to bring its thin gray light back to the valley floors. In winter, thousand-foot waterfalls freeze in mid-fall, and the shallower lakes ice to their bottoms.

Yet even in this frigid wilderness there is life: a dozen species of birds winter in the range, the caribou migrate through its passes, the wolves prowl after the caribou and high in the peaks roams half the world's remaining population of Dall sheep, some 40,000 by one recent estimate. When the sun returns to the arctic the days lengthen with astonishing rapidity, growing by nearly a quarter of an hour daily. With it comes relative warmth; the thermometer reaches as high as the 70s in July on rare occasions. There is no spring. Summer arrives suddenly late in May. The ice goes out of the rivers in one of nature's most awesome spectacles. "Water began to flow everywhere," wrote Diamond Jenness, a young archeologist stranded near Prudhoe Bay in 1913. "New birds appeared. . . . The rivers broke out all along the coast; their roar could be heard twenty miles away and their dark waters, newly exposed to light, reflected the somberness of the sky above. . . ." In the mountains, the waterfalls once again cascade and the caribou move back through to the north. The summer sun melts the top few inches of the tundra and billions of mosquitoes appear over the boggy, poorly drained land. The permafrost beneath the topsoil keeps the water from sinking in. Travel for man is difficult across the spongy land and the weather is damp and unpredictable. It can snow in July.

Still, those who have lived in the arctic for any length of time can be drawn to it forever. "The beauty of the arctic is not what you see, for instance, in the mountain country," says writer Jane Pender, who has worked in the arctic for several years. "It is not dramatic or striking. It is very subtle. There is a general impression that the North Slope is a wasteland. But in fact it is perhaps the last place in the world that's relatively untouched."

So far.

3. Marks of man:

The Hickel Highway

Man first came to the Alaskan arctic at least 6,000
years ago. He migrated from Asia across the Bering
Strait, then fanned out across the North American
arctic as far as Greenland. Across this span of time,
these early Eskimos lived in harmony with the cold
land of snow and ice and with the animals of sea
and land. Indeed, they became an integral part of
the arctic ecosystem—"living and taking from, dying
and giving to the environmental mass," as one
scholar so aptly puts it. With his nomadic, hunting
habits and primitive tools, it was beyond the
Eskimo's capacity to alter his environment in any
significant way. "The Eskimos have been wandering
across the arctic for centuries," notes writer Jane
Pender, "and they've never left a mark. Nothing."

Man's presence in the arctic environment began

to leave marks somewhat less than 100 years ago. First, the whalers. They arrived in large numbers, and settled largely along the coast and on the offshore islands. Their depredations were responsible for triggering a decline in whale populations, and their establishment of camps at places like Barrow and Beechey Point encouraged the nomadic Eskimos to concentrate in villages. The big marks were left much later during World War II when the U.S. government decided to dispatch crews to explore the 23-million-acre Naval Petroleum Reserve No. 4 (commonly referred to as NPR4 or Pet 4) for more oil. Also in the early 1940s, contractors arrived to build the Barrow Naval Station.

What happened then is a classic example of technological blundering in an alien environment. An oil exploration base was built inland at Umiat and the arctic was invaded, for the first time, by heavy tracked vehicles used to haul the drillers' equipment and supplies. The impact of that operation was described in a letter written not long ago by a man who was there:

". . . . The arctic contractors. . . . left a trail of trash and empty oil drums with scars on the prairie that haven't begun healing yet all across the Pet 4 naval reserve. They were scared people. Afraid of the land, here for the money and never intending to see it again in most cases. It was true of the Coast and Geodetic Survey crews that followed. Some of their camps were abandoned as if ahead of an invad-

ing army. When they left Pilt Point, the dishes
were left on the table!. . . ."

With equal dismay, Jane Pender observes that
"at Umiat there are piles of junk and oil barrels
that almost look like skyscrapers from the air . . .
They did some oil exploration at Wainwright
where they used heavy equipment in the summer.
Now instead of cat trails, you have vast gullies.
Essentially the land just disappears."

Though much was learned from the Pet 4 experience about the hazards of operating in the arctic,
the important lessons apparently were not learned
well enough. For in the winter of 1968-69 the state
repeated many of the same mistakes in constructing
its winter road to the North Slope. Before oil was
discovered there, the last road stopped at Livengood, a village about 60 miles north of Fairbanks.
From there to the oil exploration area were hundreds of miles of virtually trackless wilderness. The
chief means of moving in men and equipment were
by air most of the year and by barge for a few weeks
in the summer when the ice pack receded from the
Beaufort Sea coast. Indeed, during the peak 12
months of North Slope activity, more tonnage was
flown to Prudhoe Bay than was flown to beleaguered
Berlin during the entire 18-month airlift in 1948-
49.

In an attempt to improve logistics, the state decided to build a road nearly 400 miles long across
the frozen land from Livengood to Sagwon on the
North Slope. The road was ordered by then Gov.

Walter J. Hickel, who shortly thereafter became secretary of the interior. His statehouse successor, Gov. Keith H. Miller, promptly named the trail the Walter J. Hickel Highway. The Hickel Highway passed as road during the winter. But the following spring, exposed permafrost began to melt and erode and soon the road looked more like a canal along much of its length. "From an environmental point of view the Hickel Highway is the biggest screwup in the history of mankind in the arctic," one enraged University of Alaska professor has said. "It goes through the worst possible area, where the most ice-rich (permafrost) soils in Alaska are located. If an oil company had done it instead of the state of Alaska, that oil company wouldn't be operating in the state today. It's an environmental outrage."

The winter road concept was the brainchild of the trucking industry, which eagerly sought a piece of the North Slope freight action. They lobbied vigorously for it, citing the precedent of winter trails plowed through remote areas in Alaska and Canada during construction of the DEW Line. And at the time, a winter haul road seemed a good idea to most people. There were some who should have known better, of course, but little public opposition to the project was expressed. On paper it looked viable. The truckers would be able to provide lower-cost transportation than the airlines and haul a much greater amount of freight as well. There was talk, too, of the truckers paying the state a toll for using the road to help offset construction cost. And even that cost didn't seem high—S & B Construction Co. of Anchorage had bid $127,750 for the job.

In the end, however, the truckers did not provide lower-cost transportation. Frigid weather, with temperatures down to -70, so delayed construction crews (who had gotten a late start anyway) that the road was open only about a month—from March 12 to April 14. During that time, 7,464 tons of freight moved over the highway. About 80 percent of that went to the oil fields. It took the big trucks about a week each way to make the run, and the cost of freight delivered to Sagwon, well short of the main Prudhoe Bay exploration area, was in the neighborhood of $240 a ton, about the same as air freight. Three Hercules air transports could have carried the same amount of cargo in the month the highway was open—and all a Hercules requires is a 5,000-foot runway at each end of the haul.

What's more, the truckers did not pay tolls and the road did not cost $127,750. The state rejected S & B's construction bid (and all others), opting to do the job itself. The rationale was that it would take a private contractor 10 days or so to get geared up for the job, whereas the state could begin immediately, and time was precious. Promised speed, however, proved wholly ephemeral. Moreover, the state highway department did not bring in the road at either the S & B bid of $127,750 or its own initial estimate of $350,000, but at $766,000. And despite this high cost, the department ignored past arctic experience, which dictated that to operate most effectively and with the least damage to the environment, the tundra itself must not be disturbed. Many winter roads had been built before in the arctic, the best of them without much damage to the environment. They were constructed by heaping snow on the tundra, compacting it into a raised berm, and using that for the road. But the state used bulldozers instead to scrape off the snow and gouge a road into the tundra. As a result, even while the road was in operation, much time was lost clearing fresh and wind-blown snow out of the roadway trench. When spring breakup came, the Hickel Highway did not last even as long as a snow berm would have. Rapidly the highway turned into a water-filled ditch as exposed permafrost melted and water from surrounding areas drained into the roadbed. One state employee complained that the Hickel Highway was a perfect example of what can happen when a project is undertaken with only development in mind. "So the taxpayers have paid whatever it cost in money and damage to the environment," he said. "To my way of thinking that is a pretty fair subsidy to the truckers, especially since most of it could have gone up in Hercs (Hercules aircraft). What I'm afraid of is they'll say that wasn't the best route after all and do exactly the same thing somewhere else."

His fears proved justified. During the winter of 1969-70, the road was reconstructed. Of necessity, it

had to be rerouted to avoid some of the areas that
had eroded badly the previous summer. The result:
two scars instead of one.

4. Gapsmanship:

Industry's rationale

The haste and shortsightedness with which the
Hickel Highway was constructed typify the initial
pell-mell scramble to get at the pool beneath the
North Slope, a black gold rush deriving from three
main sources: 1) the oil industry's anxious desire to
recoup its huge investment and get on with profit-
taking; 2) the state's eagerness to put new budget
money in its long-empty coffers, and 3) Washington's insistence that the nation would soon face an
acute petroleum shortage unless the North Slope is
tapped.

Already, the oil companies have sunk more than
$2 billion into the Slope: $900 million for the lease
rights and the rest for exploratory and development
drilling, the purchase from Japan of hundreds of
miles of 48-inch steel pipe and other preparations

for the proposed trans-Alaska oil conduit, and the much-heralded plowing of the Northwest Passage by Humble Oil's ice-breaking tanker S.S. *Manhattan*. Despite this outlay of capital the oil companies stand to profit enormously from the Prudhoe Bay field. If the industry's estimate of 12 to 15 billion barrels of recoverable oil is near the mark (and such guesses tend to be conservative), the oil has a nominal value of between $24 billion and $30 billion, based on a wellhead price of $2 a barrel. The state's share of this windfall, through production royalties and severance taxes, will be in the neighborhood of 20 percent. The oil industry will get the rest.

The state needs funds to meet a wide range of pressing social and economic problems. As a territory, Alaska languished under what former Sen. Ernest Gruening quite accurately described as 90 years of colonialism. The bill for those decades of neglect and exploitation by special interests—particularly the unmet demand for social and economic justice for Alaska's 57,000 natives—is long overdue. Yet even in its first 11 years of statehood, Alaska was unable to meet many of these needs and existed as a pauper dependent on Washington for handouts. Though the state is rich in resources besides oil (copper, coal, timber, zinc and tin among them), most Alaskans have fastened on the petroleum boom as the only source of the revenue the state requires to solve its problems.

Then, in the words of Washington's foreign policy makers, there is the "oil gap." According to Department of the Interior projections, by 1980 the U.S. will be consuming nearly 20 million barrels of crude oil a day to keep the wheels of its motor vehicles rolling, lubricate the gears of industry, and fuel homes, apartments and growing fleets of commercial and military jets. In addition, oil by-products are used to pave roads and are vital ingredients of paint, detergent, synthetic rubber, plastics, cosmetics, nylon and fertilizer. Without North Slope oil, believers in the gap theory argue, the nation would be able to produce only about two-thirds of the required 20 million barrels. The rest would have to be imported. Some oil could be had from friendly nations such as Canada or Venezuela. But most of the import—nearly 20 percent of the country's requirements—would have to come from the Middle East, which now has 80 percent of the known crude reserves in the non-Communist world. The gapsmen say the Middle East is likely to remain unstable into the 1980s. They fear the Soviet Union's interest there in the politics of adventure will grow in direct proportion to the U.S.'s increasing dependence on Middle East petroleum.

An examination of oil production and consumption trends quickly shows why these arguments are so potent. Domestic oil production, excluding the North Slope, is expected to increase slowly from just over 10 million barrels per day (bpd) in 1968 to about 13 million bpd in 1980. Consumption, meanwhile, is expected to jump from a daily 13.9

million bpd to nearly 20 million bpd. Without the North Slope oil, this would appear to indicate an increase in the crude oil deficit from 3.8 million bpd to six million bpd. Precisely how much of the deficit the North Slope could meet cannot be gauged accurately because, despite optimistic predictions, not enough is yet known about how much oil is actually there. However, a daily production rate of two million barrels—the capacity of the proposed pipeline and a level certainly well within the Slope's potential—would allow the U.S. to keep its imports at about 23 percent of total needs. Without the Slope oil, imports might rise as high as 34 percent. "North Slope oil is U.S. oil in the U.S. market," says one oil company official, appending the industry line that "it may make the U.S. no longer dependent on foreign oil." And Walter Levy, a top oil consultant, adds this note, as quoted by *Fortune*: "A world power which depends on potentially reluctant or hostile countries for food or fuel that must travel over highly vulnerable sea routes is by definition no world power."

These sentiments were echoed in the fall of 1970 by Wilson M. Laird, director of the Department of the Interior's Office of Oil and Gas, liaison channel between the federal government and the oil industry. In an article in *Alaska Industry,* a business publication, Laird maintained that interruptions in the supply of Middle East petroleum would at some point "pass from inconvenience and hardship to the deeply disturbing character of a threat to the securi-

ty of the Western World. . . . Until 1967, the
United States was in a net surplus position: that is,
it could, if need be, provide for all its oil needs by
opening up its shut-in production, even if all imports were completely cut off. However, this is no
longer true. Net imports now exceed spare capacity
by over one million barrels a day, and the gap is
widening rapidly. . . . These figures, which graph-
ically summarize the increasing dependence of the
United States upon foreign oil supply, clearly argue
the urgent necessity for rapid development of the
vast petroleum potential of the Alaska North Slope.
Without this potential being realized, the outlook
is for a rapid descent into critical dependence upon
foreign sources for the form of energy that provides
44 per cent of the nation's heat and power. . . .
Plainly, the discovery of oil reserves of the magnitude of those now indicated in the Prudhoe Bay
area can only be regarded as a Godsend by a nation
whose capability to provide for its petroleum needs
is rapidly failing. There now remains the essential
task for all concerned, to see that the magnificent
promise of today becomes the proved performance
of tomorrow."

*   *   *

EDITOR'S NOTE: Not surprisingly, such government commercials on behalf of the oil industry
prove exceedingly persuasive both in Alaska and
Washington, buttressed as they are by the powerful
petroleum lobby. But as the introduction of this
book tries to point out, the case for the "oil gap" is

not nearly so simple and clearcut as Washington and
the industry insist. Most conservationists—though
by no means all—concede the importance of Alaska's oil to the nation. They demand, of course, that
the environment not be destroyed in getting it out.
But perhaps that risk need not be taken. Perhaps a
more judicious and fairminded reading of the
economics and politics of oil would indicate the
U.S. could get along quite nicely without further
puncturing the North Slope at all.

5. Permafrost:

The ultimate obstacle

The long arctic winter is a time of misery for the
men seeking to tap the North Slope's oil riches. In
fact, it is doubtful that any industry has ever had to
contemplate work on such a large scale under such
vexing circumstances. Not surprisingly, when environmentalists describe the arctic ecosystem as "fragile" or "vulnerable," the oilmen scoff. Their word
for it is *hostile*. Either description fits. To the
unacclimated outsider, the weather is nearly in-
tolerable. Efficiency is reduced to a fraction of what
it is in more temperate climes. Frostbite is a con-
stant hazard. The winds drive the "chill factor"
right off the little charts that warn of exposure in
-40 weather with a 40-knot wind blowing. ("Great
danger," they say. "Flesh may freeze within 30 sec-
onds.") Trucks must be left running 24 hours a day

or they may be impossible to restart for days—or weeks. Metal becomes brittle and snaps. During the worst storms, which can blow for days, the oil hands sometimes must simply abandon their drilling rigs, though swaddled from head to foot in protective down parkas, coveralls and thermal underwear.

Yet it is precisely the extreme climate they find so hostile that makes the arctic likewise peculiarly vulnerable. It is just as hard on nature's healing and restorative processes as it is on the oilmen's comfort and working conditions. This is true because the sun is the source of all natural heat and light and the arctic, of course, gets little of this radiant energy. The lack of sunlight results in low plant and animal productivity and slow recovery from environmental damage. Only about 435 species of plant life exist in the Alaskan high arctic, a fraction of the vegetation found in the great temperate and tropic ecosystems. In addition, plants grow slowly, typically taking several years to gain maturity and usually reaching only a few inches in height. Since animals pick up most of their energy secondhand from plants, the low plant productivity of the arctic leads directly to low animal productivity. There is relatively little food for plant-eating animals and, in turn, there is little for the meat-eating animals that feed on the plant-eaters. Consequently, the North Slope supports fewer than 20 kinds of land mammals, compared with the dozens of species to be found in more temperate areas. And while the 360,-000 caribou that roam the Alaskan arctic may sound

like a great many, it must be remembered that they
are spread over thousands of square miles. Neither
the plants nor the animals can stand much pressure
from man, because environmental disturbances that
would be relatively slight in the warmer regions
have long-range effects in the arctic. Plant recovery
is excruciatingly slow: witness the still-visible ruts
in the tundra made by tracked vehicles a quarter of
a century ago. And because animal populations are
sparse, they can be quickly decimated by over-
hunting.

But perhaps the most serious problem resulting
from the low level of solar radiation is permafrost. It
is the cause of almost every serious engineering
problem in the arctic, and man's attempts to manip-
ulate it have triggered the region's most critical
environmental problems. The U.S. Geological Survey defines permafrost as "rock or soil material. . . .
that has remained below 0 degrees C. (32 degrees
F.) continuously for two or more years." Thus,
permafrost can be any kind of frozen subsurface
material, including gravel or solid rock, and some of
it remains stable when thawed, presenting no major
engineering problems. Much permafrost, however,
is of the so-called "ice-rich" variety—silty soil with a
high frozen-water content. Such permafrost under-
lies much of the North Slope and many areas along
the proposed route of the pipeline the Alyeska
Pipeline Service Co. (formerly the Trans-Alaska
Pipeline System) wants to build. Since the formation of permafrost is dependent on a mean annual

ground-surface temperature of 32 degrees, the most severe permafrost conditions are found on the North Slope, where the mean annual temperature is lowest. At Barrow, for instance, the permafrost is 1,300 feet deep.

Normally, only a foot or so of surface soil thaws on the North Slope. The permafrost beneath remains, in definition and in fact, frozen solid. In this state it is quite stable. But disturbing the layer of soil and vegetation that insulates the permafrost from warm summer air and solar radiation can quickly cause disaster. "Permafrost is not sacred," says Dr. Hal Peyton, formerly of the University of Alaska, now a consultant to the oil industry and one of the leading authorities on permafrost. "But," he adds, "you sure as hell have to pay attention to what you're doing if you start tampering with it."

Unfortunately, not everyone has paid attention. In his excellent book, *Animals of the North,* William Pruitt Jr. described some of the reasons why: "After I began to understand the mechanism of the taiga [sub-arctic] ecosystem it also became evident that most of modern man's activities in the taiga depended on rationales rooted in the efforts of attempting to extrapolate temperate zone traditions and techniques to the sub-arctic. We saw the pitiful results of applying the archaic homestead laws to interior Alaska and the chain-linked disasters that followed unrestrained prospecting and exploitation of minerals in the Canadian taiga. These rationales actually have their start in a lack of knowledge of plain old-fashioned natural history." As a Geological Survey professional paper on permafrost points out, "The simple passage of a tracked vehicle that destroys the vegetation mat is enough to upset the delicate balance and to cause the top of the permafrost layer to thaw. This thawing can cause differential settlement of the surface of the ground, drainage problems, and severe frost action. Once the equilibrium is upset, the whole process can feed on itself and be practically impossible to reverse. However, if a structure is founded on permafrost that remains frozen, the frozen ground provides rocklike bearing strength."

In short, it is essential to keep permafrost frozen, thus avoiding the worst effects of thawing and at the same time taking advantage of its qualities as a foundation material. The penalty for not heeding this dictum can be costly indeed. It can lead to surface subsidence, slumping and erosion of the type that took place in Naval Petroleum Reserve No. 4 and that is occurring now along the route of the Walter J. Hickel Highway. The Geological Survey report maintains: ". . . In most areas where roads or buildings are constructed on permafrost, the procedures that cost the least in the long run are those that disturb the natural environment the least and, therefore, are conservation-oriented. Generally, the initial capital investment is greater when correct procedures are used; however, maintenance cost is considerably less. If improper procedures are used, expensive maintenance cost far exceeds the additional expense of the initial investment, and in some cases structures are damaged to the extent that they become unusable after just a few months or years. The financial losses caused by such problems as impassable roads, unusable airstrips, or damaged machinery in buildings which have settled differentially can be extremely high."

From the standpoint of securing industry cooperation in protecting the environment of Alaska, then, the best engineering and conservation practices are also clearly the cheapest. This is in marked contrast to other parts of the world, where shoddy development practices can sometimes be used to cut costs without any direct financial ill effects to the company concerned. Not so in the arctic, where the land always fights back. Unfortunately, considerable damage already has been done to the tundra in the initial exploration rush. Repairing it will be costly and may, in fact, prove ultimately impossible.

6: Sewage and Silt:

More marks of man

Behind almost every prefabricated work camp on
the North Slope is a lagoon. Into it flow kitchen
and bath water and raw sewage from toilets. The
lagoons are frozen during the winter. But in the
summer, as one oilman understated it, "They're a
bit more of a problem." And that is the current state
of the art of sewage disposal on the North Slope.

Though advances are being made—treatment facilities have been installed at a few of the larger
camps—the waste situation remains highly unsatis-
factory. Elsewhere, one obvious solution would be
the septic tank, but, again, a northern environment
precludes conventional solutions. Septic tanks cannot be used because sewage will not sink into the
ground: permafrost gets in the way. Nor can the
Slope's rivers and streams be used to carry away

human waste. "That's kind of archaic in this day and age," says Dr. R. Sage Murphy, director of the Institute of Water Resources at the University of Alaska. Besides, as Murphy and others explain, though the upper layer of tundra becomes boggy in the summer, fresh water, paradoxically, is scarce in Alaska's arctic zone. The North Slope receives no more than six or seven inches of precipitation a year and about 80 percent of that runs off during spring breakup.

With its fetid lagoons an increasing health hazard, the oil industry now seeks to modify its disposal practices. On the drill sites, oil companies plan to cover the lagoons with gravel to insulate them and keep them frozen. "But," says Warren McFall of the Federal Water Quality Administration (FWQA) in Anchorage, "we're concerned that this may cause health problems. Apparently certain organisms can survive at low temperatures for a long period of time. There is concern among microbiologists that they might be uncovered in the future." This view is supported by Dr. James Anderegg, director of the state's Division of Environmental Health, who notes that if germs are frozen they remain germs nonetheless. "The state definitely does not consider pits for sewage to be acceptable," he says. In addition, lagoon disposal presents a serious water pollution threat. Cases in which the drinking water for a North Slope camp becomes polluted by sewage from a nearby lagoon are not uncommon.

To FWQA's McFall, the answer to the sewage problem lies in the destruction of wastes—the removal of solids from liquid and their incineration. Murphy also believes incineration will prove the best way of disposing of sewage residue under the unusual working conditions in arctic Alaska. He has designed a portable unit that could be moved from site to site by truck as camp locations are changed. The oil companies, too, have been doing some research on incineration units. In the meantime, federal and state agencies are working on operational guidelines for the Slope that likely would outlaw lagoon disposal. Incineration, of course, will prove more costly but, as FWQA's Ray Morris points out, "Pollution control must be considered as a cost of doing business. We as individuals pay to have our garbage hauled away. It's only fair that a certain percentage of business income should go for pollution control."

Disposal of the trash and garbage that accumulate at any industrial site is also a difficult problem in the arctic, where the land is flat and largely featureless. It is impossible here for man to hide his debris. A single oil drum looks enormous on the open tundra and can be visible for miles. A garbage dump cannot be disguised as anything else. Nor do the examples set by military and civilian government agencies at Barrow, in Naval Petroleum Reserve No. 4 and on Amchitka Island in the Aleutians inspire much confidence. The Barrow area is littered with junk. Pet 4 has towering pyramids of unsightly trash, particularly in the Umiat area. And when the military pulled out of Amchitka after World War II, it left everything behind—thousands of Quonset huts, the carcasses of wrecked airplanes, and tons of trash that was simply bulldozed off a cliff. The junk still litters the cliff face and the shoreline below.

The damage is not limited to aesthetics. One man who has spent much of his life in the arctic gives this description of what is happening in Pet 4: "The oil drums left by the arctic explorers are rusting through now. Some were full, some had only a few cups full of fuel, but as each rusts through it is like a time bomb that kills what is in its. . . . area. Even now, 25 years later, many men who long ago left the arctic still kill wildlife with the partially empty fuel drums they left behind. If conditions are right, they may wipe out an acre or two or, with luck, a whole small lake."

To avoid such criticism, most of the oil companies have cut down drastically on the number of oil drums they haul to the Slope. Instead, they import their fuel oil in bulk and pump it into large rubber storage tanks. Initially, some of the tanks split, spilling thousands of gallons of heating oil or jet fuel. But that problem now seems in hand, and as an extra precaution the tanks are newly surrounded by dikes to contain spills.

For the most part, the drilling sites and work camps are conspicuously neat and might well be emulated at the countless industrial sites that blight most of the country's major cities. Drilling materials, casing pipe and other supplies are carefully stacked on gravel pads. There is little litter, and cleanup crews work hard to keep it that way. Atlantic Richfield began a cleanup program in 1969 that lasted several months. Crews patrolled its leases one square mile at a time, collecting all the debris in sight and loading it onto pallets. These were then moved out by helicopter and consolidated in one place for disposal. One contractor doing road construction work for the oil companies filled several thousand oil drums and buried them as part of his road's foundations. British Petroleum (BP) and ARCO used thousands of drums to help stabilize a gravel spit constructed at Prudhoe Bay as a dock for unloading supplies brought in by barge in the summer. And thousands more drums were flown back from the Slope by BP.

Another problem posed by arctic oil development is the widespread mining of gravel. The gravel lining the beds and banks of North Slope rivers is important not only to some fish, which lay their eggs in it, but to the water quality. In some cases, in fact, removal of gravel can cause disastrous silting. At the same time the gravel is enormously important to the oil industry. It is the only material generally available to provide effective insulation over permafrost for constructing roads, supply storage areas, pads for drilling rigs, and airports. It is essential to industry operations, and importing the necessary quantities from elsewhere would be prohibitively expensive, if not impractical.

Most of the millions of cubic yards of gravel the oil companies have already used on the Slope has come from its rivers, particularly the Saga-vanirktok, though some has been taken from offshore islands in the Beaufort Sea. No one is certain to what extent gravel removal has harmed such fast-flowing streams as the Sag, nor does any-one know the exact number and variety of fish that inhabit these waters. "There is nothing that says fish are especially bothered as long as the whole stream isn't tampered with," says Dr. Hal Peyton. "The gravel operators don't load the whole river with silt all at once. Silt in the rivers is a small amount. They don't borrow from open streams. They go to a bar and mine the bar. There is very little water contamination that I've seen. The other thing is that the people who are worried about the fish can't tell us anything about the fish. They don't know what species are there, whether they are anad-romous (migratory) or where their spawning ar-eas are." Bryan Sage, British Petroleum biologist, suggest that "perhaps the gravel problem is being inflated out of proportion. Let's face it, there's billions of tons of it there." Sage also says that the ability of the river to replenish its bottom gravel "far exceeds the efforts to remove it" and points out that in its delta area, where most gravel is taken, the river usually changes course substantially every spring. Fish and Game Department biologists readi-ly admit that not much is known about the Sag and other North Slope rivers. But this in itself—as many conservationists have pointed out—is reason enough for restricting the taking of gravel, at least for the time being.

The problems of sewage, litter and gravel-taking should not be minimized. Still, by far the most serious threat posed by the oil industry to the delicate Alaskan environment isn't any one of these. It's oil pollution—from the trans-Alaska pipeline and tanker operations.

7. The pipeline:

Some unanswered questions

Nothing so clearly dramatizes the environmental
crisis oil has brought to Alaska as the $1.5 billion,
800-mile pipeline the industry seeks to lay down between Prudhoe Bay and the ice-free port of Valdez
on Prince William Sound. Moving south from the
oil fields, the 48-inch pipe would cross the North
Slope to the Brooks Range along the Sagavanirktok
River, snake up through the Dietrich Pass, then
down the South Slope and across to the Yukon
River near Stevens Village. After crossing the Yukon, it would pass near Fairbanks and then generally parallel the Alaska and Richardson highways to
Valdez, en route winding through Thompson Pass.
Initially 500,000 barrels of oil a day would flow
from the wells in the artic to the tankers waiting at
Valdez. The eventual capacity, however, would be

two million barrels per day. This oil comes out of the ground under natural pressure at a temperature of about 140 degrees F. Pumping friction, supplied by 12 stations along the route, would keep the oil at about this heat all the way to its destination.

The prospect of so much hot oil coursing across the state every day poses an immeasurable threat to Alaska's environment. Even the industry's efforts to minimize that threat create hazards. For example, the oilmen had planned to bury the pipeline along 90 percent of the route. They argued that this would eliminate it as an eyesore, keep it from blocking migrating caribou and make it impossible for bored hunters or outright saboteurs to take pot shots at the pipeline. How much of the pipeline can be successfully buried, however, is a matter of considerable debate. The Department of the Interior maintains that as much as half of it will have to run above ground since much ice-rich permafrost exists along the route—merely digging a trench in such soil upsets the ecological balance.

Yet whether to construct the pipeline above or below ground seems altogether an academic question. Either way, the potential for disastrous oil spills is enormous. For one thing, the pipeline would cross seven earth fault zones, three of them highly active. Hundreds of earthquakes hit Alaska every year. Most of these are too weak to be felt, but by no means all. Tremors causing substantial ground motion occur often and on occasion can be devastating. The 1964 Alaska earthquake took 115 lives and caused $300 million in damage, much of it to Valdez, the proposed terminus for the pipeline.

In order to build the pipeline north of the Yukon River, the industry consortium, the Alyeska Pipeline Service Co. (ALPS), first must construct an access road through the now trackless area. The state has been pushing ALPS to meet secondary highway standards so the road can be used as a public highway. The possibility has thus been raised of opening a vast amount of wilderness to the certainties of litter, man-made forest fires, the scarring of terrain by four-wheel-drive vehicles and increased hunting pressure on several species of game. To accommodate the access road and work areas, the pipeline company seeks a right-of-way 100 feet wide. Outside the right-of-way there will be perhaps 30 major gravel pits to supply the huge amounts of gravel needed for road and pipeline construction.

For its part, the industry insists that the pipeline is the only presently feasible and economic way of moving the oil to market. Moreover, the oilmen maintain that pipelines have a good safety record. And they see this pipeline as the only practical way of retrieving their heavy investment in the Slope and then making a profit on their new find. Predictably, Alaska businessmen tend to look on the pipeline as a panacea, a source of hundreds of jobs and the funnel through which millions of dollars will pour into business and government budgets, increasing profits and possibly lowering taxes. They have shown little concern about the potential problems associated with construction of the pipeline. They want federal government approval of it so construction can start. As early as the summer of 1969, when even the oil industry was nowhere near ready to begin construction, John Kelsey of Valdez, then chairman of the state chamber of commerce, urged Interior Secretary Walter J. Hickel to grant speedy approval of the pipeline right-of-way and called on Alaskans to make their views known to the secretary by telegram. "Now is the time for Alaskans to stand up and be counted," Kelsey said. "It's highly important that the permit be granted. It's reached the time when if they can't get started it will delay the project for one year. . . . We're talking about tremendous amounts of money." He said that if there were "good reasons" for the delay, Hickel should make them known. As a result, Hickel was deluged with wires urging immediate construction of the project.

Conservationists, on the other hand, fear the pipeline would despoil thousands of acres of virgin wilderness, change the ecology of huge tracts, pollute Alaska's rivers and harbors and interrupt the migration patterns of the caribou herds. Many want construction delayed until all questions regarding it are answered to their satisfaction; some would like to prevent the pipeline from *ever* being built.

Meanwhile, the Interior Department, working primarily through the Bureau of Land Management (BLM) and the U.S. Geological Survey, has been asking the industry for information on how the

pipeline will be built. In the summer of 1969, the
department sent the Trans-Alaska Pipeline System,
subsequently reorganized and renamed Alyeska, a
list of 79 questions concerning the pipeline. In a
covering letter to TAPS Chairman R. E. Dulaney,
Russell Train, then under secretary of interior,
said the list was "designed to indicate the kind of
questions to which satisfactory answers will be required before permits can be given for the use of
public lands." More such questions would be forthcoming in the future, he indicated. "The secretary
has expressed the view that the oil development in
Alaska must be consistent with 'wise conservation,'" Train wrote. "We continue to affirm this
viewpoint. Our direction and emphasis will be
guided by the President's charge that the oil resources of Alaska be explored and developed 'without
destruction and with minimum disturbance.' The
enclosed and future sets of questions, as well as
discussions originating out of them, will reflect this
commitment. With the conviction that proper environmental and social safeguards are coordinate, and
not competitive, with industrial development, it
would be helpful to us, in our anticipation of industry's timetables, to have your initial reply within four weeks."

The reply came back in nine days. In a covering
letter to Train, Dulaney said that TAPS concurs
"that our project should be constructed consistent
with wise conservation and reiterate our earlier
observation that good pipeline design dictates design

and construction procedures that will cause a minimum disturbance to the natural environment. Since we start from a common position, it is to be expected that the details of our proposed development will be consistent with sound conservation principles." Attached to the covering letter was a 20-page document outlining the planning and research that TAPS had done to that point in preparing for construction of the pipeline. So far, the response maintained, TAPS had initiated a seismic study of pipeline and terminal facilities by Dames & Moore, a geological consulting firm; a prototype test facility at Barrow consisting of 1,100 feet of 42-inch pipe "laid under varying conditions to determine stresses developed due to freezing soil and ice formation"; a geological investigation of the proposed Yukon River crossing; a research program conducted by the University of Alaska to determine the best methods of revegetating damaged tundra; a geological and permafrost study along the pipeline route, and marine ecology and geological studies of the terminal site at Valdez. The pipeline company said that only the most modern engineering techniques would be used in constructing the conduit and that these would make the chances of a major spill occurring negligible. Should such a spill occur, TAPS said, it would be prepared to control it quickly by "providing block valves at major water crossings to shut off drainage" and "having crews and equipment available to localize, contain and dispose of spill and to clean up the area." More specifically, TAPS said that the flow of crude oil to a break would be controlled and reduced by:

1. "Gravity drainage to tankage at any pump station whenever this is feasible. This, of course, depends on the location of the break and the pump stations on either side of the break."

2. "Isolation of the broken section—first, by immediate closure of remotely controlled block gates at the existing pump stations; second, by immediately proceeding to the break area and closing the main line block gate on the up-stream or uphill side of the break. . ."

3. "Equipment and repair crews will move in immediately to prevent spread of the oil by using dikes and dams. The break will be sealed off using clamps and sleeves designed for this purpose. The oil will be recovered or disposed of and all damages corrected." The TAPS re-ply to the Interior Department questions also reaffirmed that "currently, it is anticipated that approximately 95 per cent of the pipeline will be buried and the above-ground portions will be in relatively short sections. Consequently no significant barriers to migration routes of mammals is anticipated. However, where neces-sary, ramps or underpasses will be provided to ensure adequate passageways for migrating mammals."

Of major concern to biologists has been the man-ner in which the pipeline would be put across rivers—particularly the Yukon. A winter break there under ice several feet thick could do incalculable damage to the river and its fisheries. TAPS told the Interior Department:

". . . all river crossings including the Yukon are presently planned as underwater crossings. Where danger of scour exists, the pipeline will be weighted with concrete and placed in a ditch excavated in the bedrock where possible or well below the active river bottom. The proposed Yukon crossing will be placed in bedrock. Initial investigation indicated that major rivers can be crossed during the winter time with little or no injury to fish and water birds. Construction will be scheduled to cause the least amount of disturbance in this area consistent with the character of the stream crossed."

Though additional exchanges have occurred, the pipeline company, as Secretary Hickel repeatedly pointed out, still had not answered all relevant questions to the Interior Department's satisfaction by the end of 1970. When and if it does, and the right-of-way and construction permits are granted, construction and operations will be governed by a set of Interior Department stipulations coordinated by the Bureau of Land Management. The stipulations contain the provision that "an advance right of construction permit should not be granted until a formal application showing the exact route of the pipeline is submitted." By the fall of 1970, no such detailed application had been forthcoming. In ex-

plaining the necessity for this provision, the BLM
said that "considerable resource damages have already been incurred due to past exploratory work.
The Bureau must be staffed and prepared to super-
vise this construction to prevent indiscriminate development of trails, access roads, heliports, pipe
storage areas and crossing of streams." Other key
stipulations:

1. The pipeline company is required to sub-
mit "a contingency plan for oil spill control,
disposal and cleanup. . . . The contingency
plan shall include separate, specific oil spill
cleanup techniques for (a) terrestrial, (b)
lake, (c) stream and (d) estuary and tideland
spills. The plan must be acceptable and approved by [the BLM] prior to pumping oil
through the pipeline."

2. Wastes to be collected and disposed of
"include human waste, trash, garbage, tissue,
various liquid, equipment and miscellaneous
solid wastes."

3. The pipeline company is required to recognize the right of the BLM "to close to
pipeline and road construction certain areas
for periods of time. . . . to protect wildfowl
nesting activities, concentration of migrating
fish and wildlife and crucial feeding, spawning
and rearing areas. Closure to construction may
also be ordered within the permit area . . . for
reasons connected with hunting and fishing
and protection of fish and wildlife resources."

4. "The design of all pipeline and auxiliary facilities shall be reviewed and approved prior to any construction."

5. The pipeline is to be constructed "in such a manner as to minimize permafrost degradation. This stipulation shall apply to all pipeline construction, whether buried or installed above grade."

6. "Construction vehicles shall not be driven outside the boundaries of the right-of-way and access roads at any time" except when approved by the BLM.

7. The company "shall not disturb the surface vegetative cover on the tundra north of the Brooks Range summit. Scraping, blading, ripping and other disturbances by mechanical equipment shall not be allowed except when absolutely necessary to construct a trench for pipe burial and drilling of holes for piling."

8. The pipeline firm "shall seed, plant and fertilize all lands requiring revegetation with a mixture containing adaptable grass species."

The BLM also made it clear that the pipeline company would be required to comply with any new regulations or stipulations that might be developed as work progressed. The BLM noted that this would be necessary because "preliminary design of the pipeline, routing, etc., leave many questions unanswered. In addition, the abundance and distribution of fish, wildlife, forest and range resources as well as their reaction to problems im-

posed by oil development and pipeline operations
are poorly understood." In explaining the purpose
of the proposed stipulations, the BLM dealt with
the type of environmental damage uncontrolled
construction could do—and in some cases already
has done. For instance: "Numerous heliports have
been constructed indiscriminately during the preliminary route exploration phase, resulting in many
barren scars along the route. Considerable erosion
damage can result if construction of heliports and
access roads to them are not controlled. Apparently
the permittee was not aware of the fact that a special
land use permit was required." The BLM also
cautioned that:

1. "It is a common practice for equipment
operators and maintenance mechanics to drain
oil and fuels from equipment directly onto
ground surface as well as to throw away used
oil and fuel filters in a similar manner. Water
contamination results from such practices and
should be prevented."

2. "Pollution of a stream system by various
construction activities or by pipeline breaks or
leaks could destroy important spawning
grounds hundreds of miles downstream."

3. "Pollution of the natural waters along the
pipeline route cannot be tolerated. Here we
have an opportunity to protect waters that are
in a pristine condition. We must not find ourselves in a situation where we will be required
to perform expensive watershed and pollution

projects to return the stream to natural quality. Many lessons have been learned in the problems of water pollution in our society. We must make the effort not to repeat the same mistakes."

4. "Those sections [of the pipeline] constructed above ground could be an effective barrier to caribou and other big game movements. . . . There is no evidence to support the supposition that caribou will pass under an elevated pipe or, for that matter, over a ramp."

5. "Selection of the Dietrich-Antigun River route in preference to Anaktuvuk Pass will not solve caribou problems from the point of avoiding major migration routes. Anaktuvuk Pass is rated as a major migration route simply because people live there and more work has been done in that area. The Dietrich, head of the Chandalar, and Sagavanirktok rivers are reported in federal aid reports as having major concentrations or movements of caribou. Trails now existing in this area show very heavy use."

6. "The damage of siltation and oil spillage is potentially much greater than loss of habitat or disturbance through construction."

7. "In many cases irreparable damage occurs where vehicles or equipment are driven across the tundra and permafrost. Past traffic across the tundra and permafrost is still very evident. The natural resources losses in this case

amount to more than the cost of the pipeline,
due to the loss in soil productivity, vegetative
cover, wildlife forage, stream siltation, water
pollution, and soil loss."

8. "Surface disturbance of the tundra and
permafrost must be held to a minimum because rehabilitation methods are not known at
the present time. Observations of past tundra
and permafrost degradation is slowly continu-
ing. Many of the disturbed areas have become
erosion channels; subsidence has occurred;
lakes, ponds and bogs have formed."

These are only some of the questions the federal
government is asking the oil industry. Clearly, they
raise two additional ones. Can the oil companies
meet these rigid stipulations and still build an
economically viable pipeline? And even if they can,
is it at all possible to make an 800-mile pipeline
across Alaska environmentally safe?

8. The passage:

Supertankers—superspills

For nearly 400 years, men dreamed of a Northwest Passage joining East and West. Though dozens
of adventurers set out to find that fabled passage,
none succeeded until 1905, when Norwegian explorer Roald Amundsen and his small crew completed a three-year transit around the top of Canada
in a wooden sloop. After that, a handful of other
surface ships (and many United States nuclear sub-
marines) traversed the frigid water route. But man
was still unable to turn this iceway into a commer-
cially profitable trade route for merchant ships.

Then came the S.S. *Manhattan.*

In 1968, the Humble Oil and Refining Company
committed itself to a $50-million experiment with
the 115,000-ton tanker, the largest United States-
flag merchant ship. To conquer the passage, Hum-

ble converted the *Manhattan* into the world's most powerful icebreaker. In the summer of 1969, the ship crunched her way through the ice to determine if still larger 250,000-ton icebreaking tankers would be practical moving oil from the North Slope to the United States East Coast. It was an experiment which aroused the most intense interest among oilmen, government officials and conservationists, involving, as it did, considerable technological achievement, imagination and daring—as well as some ominous portents for the environment.

The *Manhattan* was chosen because her 43,-000-horsepower plant was nearly one and one-half times larger than those on most other ships twice her size. And it was clear that plowing through pack ice six to 18 feet thick, and pressure ridges that might be as much as 100 feet thick, was going to require prodigious power. The ship, then seven years old, was cut into four pieces at the Sun Shipbuilding & Dry Dock Company at Chester, Pennsylvania. Sun kept the stern section. The original bow was put into storage until another conventional hull could be built for it. The forward section of the hull, including the No. 1 oil tank, was sent to Newport News Shipbuilding & Dry Dock Company in Virginia, and the midsection went to the Alabama Ship Building & Dry Dock Company at Mobile.

While the three hull sections were being fitted with heavy protective belts of steel plate (which increased the *Manhattan's* beam 16 feet to 148 feet), the Bath Iron Works in Maine built a new icebreaking bow, which added 65 feet to the vessel's length. The new bow was designed to attack the ice at a sharp 18 degree angle, rather than the 30 degree angle of most traditional icebreaker bows. In addition, the bow was made 16 feet wider than the rest of the hull so the ship's hard nose could break a wide path in the ice, allowing much cleaner, more friction-free passage for the hull through the ice. When the work was done, the *Manhattan* had an additional 9,000 tons of steel in strategic places. She also was much more sensitive. Hundreds of tiny pressure gauges were installed along the hull to tell scientists and engineers what forces were at work on the ship in varying ice conditions. Closed circuit television was installed to monitor ice flow around the ship. Two helicopters were put aboard to scout the route ahead of the vessel, gather ice cores for analysis aboard ship and collect information with infrared film and laser beams. Small computers aboard stored all data gathered for analysis and study later. From the outset, Humble said that even if the *Manhattan* herself couldn't break through the worst ice encountered, she should be able to collect all the data necessary to determine whether the larger 250,000-ton ships would be practical. "Our primary purpose is to obtain the additional information necessary to design ice-worthy new tankers for year-round operations," said Captain Roger A. Steward, skipper of the *Manhattan*. "We're counting on tonnage and horsepower to smash through the ice ridges." The *Manhattan* did just that. Then she carried back to the East Coast a single, symbolic barrel of North Slope oil.

But there were some disquieting incidents during the historic voyage. On the westward trip, the *Manhattan* had been doing so well that Humble decided to test her under the worst conditions that could be found. Humble found them by deliberately taking the ship into the ice-choked McClure Strait, where wind and currents combine to accumulate some of the oldest, hardest and thickest ice in the northern Canadian islands. Not long after entering the strait, the ship became trapped and could move neither forward nor back in the thick ice. So the huge ship sat helpless for several hours until an accompanying icebreaker finally freed her.

The seriousness of this incident was not revealed until late 1970, when two participating United States Coast Guard officers, Captain F.A. Goettel and Lieutenant Commander A.D. Super, published a little-noted report in the Marine Technology Society Journal. They wrote that the United States and Canadian governments contributed substantial help to the project, including ice reconnaissance flights by United States Navy planes over the Beaufort Sea for six months before the voyage, and establishment of an ice-forecasting system in cooperation with Canada. Several exotic instruments were used on scouting flights ahead of the *Manhattan*, including a laser geodolite, an infrared scanner, high resolution aerial cameras and side-looking airborne radar (SLAR), which played a key role in the rescue of the tanker. The authors reported that the *Manhattan* "unknowingly entered a vast flow of multi-year ice and became beset, unable to move forward or astern" in the McClure Strait. In this condition, with icebreakers at first unable to get her out, the *Manhattan* was in danger of being carried aground by the moving ice. A SLAR reconnaissance was flown, and the information gathered was then dropped to the ship. The radar data showed an escape route. Thus was the vessel freed. Because of this experience, the authors reported, long-range reconnaissance and ice-forecasting would have to be provided by the United States and Canadian governments if the Northwest Passage were to be used as a commercial shipping route. In addition, icebreakers would have to stand by for rescue duty.

On the way home, the tanker had another difficult encounter with ice. It resulted in a puncture in one of the oil tanks (filled only with sea water ballast) "big enough to drive a truck through." Humble said the hole was in an unprotected part of the hull which would be armored with heavier plating in other specially designed icebreaking tankers. Yet many arctic veterans remain skeptical that any type of icebreaking tanker, no matter how big or powerful, can make the Northwest Passage a year-round trade route. They point out that it was summer when the *Manhattan* made her voyage, and ice conditions then were the least difficult in years.

One of the skeptics is Captain Joseph Barnard,

an arctic explorer who sailed the north at the turn
of the century. Barnard predicted that the *Manhattan* was unlikely to have much trouble in the passages between Canada's northern islands. "There's
deep water in them and the currents that work
through them keep the ice conditions better for
navigation," he said. "But when they come out of
these channels and get into the arctic itself it's a
different story. And things are never the same out
there from one time to the next. Out there the sea
is shallower and the floes get bigger and thicker—
unbelievably bigger and thicker. I remember the
season of 1913 out there when we had practically
one solid floe that was 20 feet from the surface of
the sea to the top of the ice sheet. That means there
was either 150 or more feet under the surface or it
was anchored fast to the bottom. Nothing that man
can make can break ice like that . . . They probably
can get through once in a while . . . But I don't
think they'll ever be able to make it a regular route
for [tanker] traffic."

By late 1970, following a second summer excursion by the *Manhattan,* Humble had virtually decided that it would be impractical to construct
larger icebreaking tankers. In addition to the ice
hazards, Humble understandably backed off for economic reasons as well.

There is yet another problem: the shallowness of
the sea off the North Slope. The continental shelf
there runs so far out that any tanker terminal
would probably have to be located at least 30 miles

offshore. Clearly, such a facility would be enormously expensive to construct. And once built, it would
be fully exposed to the infrequent, but violent arctic
storms that can howl for days in the winter and com-
press the pack ice against the shore with incredible
force. The prospect of a 250,000-ton tanker being
crushed by the ice and spilling a million barrels of
crude oil into the Beaufort Sea continues to give
environmentalists and wildlife experts nightmares.
The result, they fear, could be even worse than such
disasters as Santa Barbara and the *Torrey Canyon*.
Ray Morris of the FWQA notes that tankers "have
one of the best safety records in shipping. But when
they do have trouble it's almost a national disaster."

Any major oil spill in those arctic waters almost
certainly would have detrimental effects on
bowhead whales, many of which migrate into the
Beaufort Sea in the spring and spend the summer
there, feeding on the abundant supply of microscop-
ic plant and animal life; on polar bears, which
prowl the coast and ice pack year-round in search of
seals; on ring, bearded and harbor seals, which feed
on the crustaceans found in the arctic waters, and
on the various plankton and crustaceans, which
form the beginning of the arctic's short, vulnerable
marine food chain. "I shudder to think what would
happen if you lost a 250,000-ton tanker," says biologist Jim Brooks. "It would gum up the coast of
Alaska and Canada so bad that sea birds, marine
mammals and vertebrates in the beach zone would

be disastrously affected. The oil would be confined by the ice and couldn't spread and dissipate." Polar bears would be in trouble because "an oily polar bear is going to be a cold polar bear. The oil will destroy the insulation of his pelt and he probably won't survive. . . . The possibility of oil spills is something that should cause everyone involved to build in every safeguard and precaution before-hand. It's probable, however, that accidents are going to happen no matter what precautions are taken. In fact there's no question about it."

Dr. Charles Behlke of the University of Alaska, an aggressive booster of North Slope oil develop-ment, concedes that "we are going to have to face the possibility that something is going to go wrong. We're going to have to expect a catastrophe." But in the long run, he adds, "With the appropriate controls, offshore pollution is not going to be a problem." He is confident that the required technol-ogy can be developed. "If tankers such as the *Manhattan* can push their way through the ice, they should be able to withstand the winter storms. Structures can be built that would make it possible to have ice protection the year round. There isn't a damn thing up there that can't be solved."

But what would happen if a tanker did break up in the ice? Some ideas were provided in a paper prepared for the Canadian Wildlife Service by Dr. Richard E. Warner, professor of environmental biol-ogy at the Memorial University of Newfoundland. Professor Warner reported that the rate of biological decomposition of crude oil is dependent on temperature. "The decomposition rate slows markedly at lower temperatures, and at 0 degrees C. [32 degrees F.] is drastically reduced, some components of the process stopping altogether," Professor Warner warned. He added that "decomposition in the arctic oceans, whose temperatures are at 0 degrees C., or below, throughout the year, would be very slow indeed. Where oil is exposed to still lower temperatures, for instance when carried onto shorelines and ice floes, biochemical decay would be virtually nonexistent, and the oil would persist for decades, perhaps centuries."

The problems of tanker operations at Valdez, the terminus of the proposed trans-Alaska pipeline, would seem less severe than those associated with the Beaufort Sea, but they remain acute. Valdez is an ice-free port, thus eliminating one major problem. Its harbor is also sufficiently deep to accommodate supertankers with no trouble: the bigs ships would not be totally exposed to storms while loading. And the storms at Valdez, while sometimes bitter, seldom display the unbridled ferocity of those in the arctic. However, a tanker can't sail empty to the terminal where it takes on its cargo of oil. It would ride too far out of the water and be unstable. So its tanks must be filled with sea water ballast.

But a tanker's cargo tanks are never completely emptied when it is unloaded. Consequently, the ballast water becomes "dirty"—contaminated with crude oil from the last cargo. And ballast must be disposed of before a new cargo of oil can be put aboard.

This frequently is where trouble starts. It has not been uncommon in the past for tanker captains to dump dirty ballast in areas where they thought they could get away with it.

Most new tankers have tank-cleaning facilities that remove most residual oil before ballast is taken aboard. And some modern vessels have tanks that are used for ballast alone, not oil. Yet this does not apply to all ships by any means, and a supertanker of the type the oil companies plan to bring into Valdez could be carrying hundreds of thousands of barrels of water contaminated by as much as a few thousand barrels of oil. Pumping that amount of oily ballast into the Valdez harbor could have disastrous effects.

To cope with this problem, the Alyeska Pipeline Service Company plans to install extensive ballast and bilge water treatment facilities ashore. "All oil ballast water arriving in tankers at the southern terminal will be pumped ashore and passed through separators to extract the oil, thereby ensuring that ballast will not contaminate waters adjacent to the terminal," ALPS has told the Interior Department. After this treatment, the ballast would be pumped into the harbor. But even such treated ballast could cause problems. "It is a delicate estuary," says Dr. R. Sage Murphy, director of the Institute of Water Resources at the University of Alaska. "Even if it is clean ballast, it came from somewhere else. It may upset the Valdez estuary biologically."

In addition to the shore treatment facilities, ALPS has told the Interior Department that it plans to utilize the latest engineering and construction techniques to insure that oil is not lost during ballast unloading and crude oil-loading operations at Valdez. The same will be true of the storage tanks, another potential source of pollution. Initially, ALPS plans to have a storage capacity of five million barrels of oil in 11 tanks. The firm has submitted to the Interior Department the rough outlines of contingency plans it will use in case an oil spill does occur.

"I don't think the problems at Valdez are as dangerous as in the arctic," says Dr. David R. Klein, head of the Cooperative Wildlife Research Unit at the University of Alaska, "but there will be a tremendous number of tankers and, as a result, a tremendous potential danger. Prince William Sound is a very important area for salmon. Cordova has an important clam fishery that definitely would be detrimentally affected by an oil spill. And there are sea otters in the area. They are particularly vulnerable to oil spills."

9. Wildlife factors:

The end of the game?

Man's invasion of the arctic is certain to have an impact on the region's wildlife resources. The process of change, in habitat and species populations, will inevitably accelerate, though in which directions no one is quite sure. Yet one can be fairly sure the directions of change will be of no great benefit to the wildlife. The hunting ethic in Alaska, for example, is very much of the old frontier—only now it is pursued from the vantage of a spotter plane or snowmobile. "Alaska," says Urban C. Nelson of The Nature Conservancy, "cannot long afford wildlife merely as a replacement for a call to the butcher for a steak."

Most wildlife specialists appear least concerned about the caribou. It is the most plentiful game animal in the arctic and seems somewhat adaptable

to the presence of man—at least so far. Oil development in the caribou's summering grounds and the
above-ground stretches of the trans-Alaska pipeline
may alter migration patterns somewhat and hunting
pressure is certain to increase. But with proper controls, the species might be able to withstand the increase of human activity. This is by no means true,
however, for more than a dozen other animals,
among them the Dall sheep, polar bear, wolverine,
wolf and Barren Ground grizzly. "I personally don't
think there is any question but that the Barren
Ground grizzly is going to go," says David M. Hickok
of the University of Alaska. "He is extremely curious and is going to be nosing around garbage dumps.
He also presents a certain menace. So he is going to
get shot. There may be 'no guns in camp,' but he's
going to get shot. Same for the wolves and the Dall
sheep."

Dr. Robert Weeden of the University of Alaska,
formerly a game biologist for the Alaska Fish and
Game Department, believes that, in addition to any
habitat changes the oil exploration causes, a major
problem will be the simple presence of a large
number of people on the North Slope. He sees no
particular problem with increased hunting pressure, however, if the Fish and Game Department
can complete inventories of the various species and
adjust hunting regulations accordingly. Yet whether
such regulations would be forthcoming is, of course,
a matter of speculation.

What's more, even the stiffest regulations would

be difficult to enforce over such a vast territory.

When oilmen talk about wildlife conservation they always stress the Kenai National Moose Range south of Anchorage. Most of them are proud of what happened there and contend it offers the strongest evidence that the oil industry can be compatible with the survival of wildife in Alaska. But does it?

The 1.7-million-acre Moose Range was rigidly zoned to protect its inhabitants. This zoning established the Andrew Simon Natural Area, a virtually trackless wilderness; the Chickaloon Flats Waterfowl Area on the north shore of the Kenai Peninsula, for waterfowl management and public hunting; the Central Public Use Area and the Intensive Resource Use Area. Only in this last zone was the petroleum industry allowed to operate, and then under the strictest regulations designed to minimize environmental damage. Watched closely by the U.S. Bureau of Sport Fisheries and Wildlife, which administers the range, the industry established an undeniably neat oil field.

As oil development proceeded in that zone, the moose population increased throughout the range from 4,000 to 7,500. The oil industry sometimes claims credit for this on the theory that more roads made travel easier for the big animals and that new growth on cutover areas provided ideal moose browse. The wildlife experts who run the range maintain, however, that no evidence supports this view Moreover, a Bureau of Sport Fisheries and

Wildlife publication points out, ". . . Experience has demonstrated . . . that the effects [of the industry's presence] include some long-term scarring of the environment, initial stream pollution from silt and debris, a potential for pollution of fish and waterfowl waters, added fire hazards, and human occupancy foreign to a natural habitat. The net result is a significant change in the environment. . . ."

Dr. David R. Klein, head of the Cooperative Wildlife Research Unit at the University of Alaska, concedes that "oil has been developed fairly compatibly on the Moose Range." But, he adds, "The reason it worked is because of the very stringent restrictions. . . . the moral is that oil development. . . . requires strict regulations." Yet even then, problems can arise. "When you reach a certain stage of development," says geologist Gerald Ganopole, "the value of the land for its original purposes disappears. The land is lost through a process of degradation. . . ."

Most important, there remains the question of how much of the Moose Range experience is transferable to the North Slope. The range presents no permafrost problems; the Slope does. The range has a much higher annual mean temperature, which encourages revegetation. The range's principal inhabitant, the moose, has proved compatible with man. How compatible the caribou will be remains to be fully tested. Moreover, the Slope is home to animals that never have lived easily with man: the wolf, the wolverine and the Barren Ground grizzly, among others.

Nor does man's record in the arctic thus far afford much encouragement to those seeking to protect its wildlife. Already, the wilderness value of a vast area has been lost, much of it within the last two years as the oil companies have dragged their technology around the North Slope. They have mined rivers and offshore islands for gravel. They have spread the gravel five feet thick over the tundra to build at least seven air strips, dozens of drilling sites and many miles of roads. They have constructed huge gravel pads on the shores of the Beaufort Sea to receive freight from barges during the summer. They have bulldozed pits and lagoons for sewage, solid wastes and garbage. In some cases, they have littered the tundra with oil drums and other trash. Though for the most part they have restricted cross-country travel during the summer months for employees and contractors, this has not been true of the seismic exploration crews. And the damage they have done merely looking for oil may exceed that done by the drilling itself.

One man intimately familiar with the North Slope gave this description of a seismic crew's operation at a lake where a pair of swans had nested every year for the past quarter-century:

"The caterpillars plowed out a landing field. The Nodwells [Canadian-built tracked vehicles] pulled the camp trailers up and the oil drums marked the landing strip. Several cargo airplanes full of freight, mostly oil drums, came in. The seismic work was done, strings of holes blown in the prairie, the trash dumped, the oil drained from the machines upon the ice, the snow drifted over it and the camp was pulled away to another lake where the operation was repeated. Summer came, the oil and trash floated on the first lake, the oil drums, some 80 strong, floated about until some washed ashore and others sank. The oil slicks killed the birds that dared to land. The swans had already left. They didn't return. The nest is empty."

In response to such attacks, the oil industry insists it did not realize in the beginning how delicate the arctic was. The industry stresses its subsequent promises to take every precaution in developing its oil fields. Toward this end, the oil companies have initiated a number of studies and projects:

• A party of scholars financed by the pipeline consortium has explored the proposed pipeline route. These investigators studied not only the mammals and fish along the route, but all biological systems, including various kinds of grasses that might be used to revegetate areas disturbed by the pipeline.

• Atlantic Richfield cleaned up its lease holdings on the North Slope, including much debris that was there when ARCO arrived. It also sponsored a "garden patch," an area of badly damaged tundra that has been seeded with 39 varieties of

grasses in an effort to find one that would take hold
and grow.

• ARCO is investigating the use of plastic to
insulate the permafrost so less gravel would have to
be scooped from North Slope rivers for roads and
drilling pads.

Beyond these programs, the industry is conducting basic research or farming special projects out
to the University of Alaska. More than a dozen
industry-sponsored studies have been launched by
University of Alaska researchers, almost all of them
with at least implied value for conservation.

Despite these and other efforts, the fact remains
that whatever safeguards the oil companies devise,
wildlife in Alaska is put in serious jeopardy by
their industrial presence. In the end, the odds that
animals and oil can coexist in the frigid northern
ecosystem seem slim indeed.

10. An arctic policy:

How government goofed

The development of Alaska's oil resources unquestionably will change the face of the state. To get the oil out without altering the land and the quality of the water is beyond man's current technological capabilities. Even in strictly controlled areas like the Kenai Moose Range, oil industry operations have caused some environmental change. Much greater changes have occurred on the North Slope and more change is inevitable. So the issue that must be faced—and faced now—is not whether there will be change, but rather what type of change it will be, what sort is desirable, how much of it is necessary if industry is to operate efficiently, how much is permissible if scenic and wilderness values are to be preserved, and in what areas it will be allowed to occur. The urgency of this task should be clear to every citizen. "I know of no major mistake made outside Alaska that hasn't been repeated here," warns Joseph H. Fitzgerald, whose tenure as head of the Federal Field Committee gave him an unusually broad insight into Alaska's problems.

The penalty for mistakes is being paid daily in the rest of the nation: in pollution of virtually every major body of water, poisoned air, scenic areas blighted by industrial waste, rotting central cities, and sprawling ticky-tacky suburbs. So far Alaska's small population and enormous size have prevented these problems from reaching the crisis level that prevails elsewhere. Yet when conservationists express their concern about what is happening to Alaska's wilderness, they frequently hear a blunt, "So what? Only a small piece of wilderness is being changed. Alaska is all wilderness. There will always be enough."

Indeed, Alaska is largely wilderness still and its territorial magnitude often does make it seem unconquerable. It sprawls across 586,400 square miles—20 percent of the area of the rest of the U.S. There are still two square miles of land for each of its 304,000 human inhabitants. It still is possible in theory to walk 500 miles in a straight line without encountering a single fence, road, airstrip—or man. But perhaps the most compelling statistic of all is this one: the land and water area of the 50 states, including Alaska, totals 2.3 billion acres. Of this, only about 10 percent remains in a truly natural state. And most of that 10 percent is in Alaska.

"I am convinced that the discovery of oil has telescoped the margin of time for wilderness preservation in Alaska into a very few years," says biologist Robert Weeden. "Consider that there is no other private industry with similar ability to amass huge amounts of capital, and move men and equipment to remote parts of the earth. Consider that there is no other industry that changes the appearance of the landscape over such large areas merely in the process of looking for a resource. Consider the extreme rapidity with which surface transportation systems can follow oil discovery, as exemplified today in the North American arctic. Consider that these roads and railroads quickly make other resource extraction and use economically feasible. Consider that the geology is favorable for commercial oil deposits under about half of Alaska, including most of the treeless areas from the Alaska Peninsula north and east to the Canadian border. Consider the desire of American oil companies to find reserves in North America that can be tapped when foreign sources are cut off. Consider, finally, that in the space of a few months oil explorations have destroyed the wilderness character of an area in northern Alaska bigger than the state of Massachusetts. I, for one, do not give our huge de facto wilderness long to survive."

Former State Rep. W. P. Kay points out that what happens in the state as its oil resources are developed will have an important influence not only on the remaining wilderness areas, but on the cities as well, because "Alaska is going to experience a great increase in population. One thing that isn't generally realized is that while Alaska is vast, the economically habitable area is not very large. It would be relatively easy for overcrowded conditions to develop."

Of course, many Alaskans, like Dr. Charles Behlke of the University of Alaska, are not so pessimistic about the environment. "I have pretty definite feelings about industrial development," he says. "If you look at New York state or California, they have a lot of heavy industry crowded in around the major cities. This makes a mess of the environment. . . It would be wonderful if you could separate this heavy industry from where you live. In Alaska we have this advantage: the heavy industry is at Prudhoe Bay where it's not going to bother anyone. It's an ideal situation. You couldn't ask for anything better. The oil companies are definitely going to make a mess of the tundra—there's no way out of it. And there is no question that there is going to be some water pollution. The character of the North Slope is going to change, but I don't think it is going to be on a scale that will ruin the entire Slope. And I don't think we should get too excited about an area that we didn't give two hoots in hell about two years ago."

From disparate views such as these, Alaska must formulate a policy with which to confront its environmental crisis. Until now, Alaska, like most other

states, has considered the problems associated with
development on an individual basis as they arose. In
the past, that may have been an adequate policy;
but those days are over. A first priority for Alaska
must be the development of a comprehensive policy
for planned development: one that takes into consideration not only the needs of efficient industrial
operation, but also the maintenance of a decent
environment, one not only fit for human habitation
but which retains its ability to lift and ennoble the
human spirit. Industry constantly repeats the dictum that its first responsibility is to its stockhold-
ers. But industry also has grave responsibilities that
extend far beyond merely guaranteeing the stock-
holder a sufficient return on his investment. In the
case of Alaska, the most obvious requirement is that
the oil industry take care of the land while getting
the oil out. The North Slope is public land. It is
part of the common heritage and belongs to all the
people—not to the oil companies and their stock-
holders. The oil companies have leased the land,
and with it the right to extract the oil beneath it.
But there is nothing in the lease agreements that
confers on the oil companies the right to ruin the
surface of the land for other purposes.

Government must become the watchdog of the
public interest, a role in which it has failed miser-
ably so far. If there is a villain in this piece, it is the
federal government, which ruled Alaska for 90 years
without ever formulating a national policy on the
arctic. There still is no such policy. And in the

nearly two years since the scope of the North Slope discovery became evident, the state government also has been negligent in providing the sort of leadership that the situation demands. What is required now is a cooperative effort between the state and federal governments to assert that leadership, and to promote development of an arctic policy that will provide guidelines for true progress in Alaska for both industry and the public interest.

The public, for its part, must demand responsible action from both government and industry. A necessary first step here is that the public ask for the information it needs to make intelligent decisions. David M. Hickok, among many others, deplores the "lack of information available to the public on the plans and operational programs of both industry and government on resource use and environmental management or preservation. Both industry and government are deliberately preventing the operation of a public forum until after the important decisions are made." Indeed, in the crucial early phase of Slope development, both industry and government were secretive to the point of absurdity on almost every aspect of the operation. The situation has improved only marginally since then. As a result, industry has operated as it pleased while that state looked on (when it looked at all) with approval, despite the obvious need for regulation in a number of areas. Much unnecessary damage has been done to the fragile environment of the Slope, and the public has been told precious little about it—in some instances, nothing at all.

The rapidity of the North Slope development took virtually everyone by surprise. And in the scramble to obtain geological data, oil companies cut corners that, from an environmental standpoint, shouldn't have been cut. That such unnecessary damage is still occurring is a direct result of the failure of government first to provide regulations for industry activity and then, after formulating them, failing to supply personnel to enforce them. The federal government, while spending millions of dollars on pure research in the Antarctic, made no similar investment, which could have been of immediate practical value, in Alaska. Thus was there no established body of knowledge on operating in the arctic. The state government was inexcusably tardy in coming up with regulations for the North Slope, though it certainly could have done so less than a year after the oil rush began in earnest (it took about 18 months.) Says conservationist Gerald Ganopole: "The only thing the state has done to date is advance development—and by development I mean it in the worst possible way: poorly controlled, poorly planned, quick methods of getting resources into private hands to the detriment of . . . . areas that could potentially merit preservation, conservation or even benefit the entire country."

Clearly, these minimum steps seem in order:

  • The establishment of a national policy on the arctic, endorsed by the president and coordinated by the National Science Foundation. Much of the groundwork necessary to devise such a policy already has been done by the Federal Field Committee for Development Planning in Alaska. Under this policy, the foundation would be responsible for coordinating all scientific research in the arctic, avoiding wasteful duplication and hastening the development of an adequate body of knowledge about operating in the arctic.

• Establishment of a central information bank on the arctic at the University of Alaska, where the rapidly growing body of arctic knowledge would be properly catalogued and indexed, available for anyone who needed it.

• Enforcement of strict state regulations concerning the use of vehicles on the tundra, the taking of gravel from streams, sanitation, water pollution, garbage and trash disposal and permafrost degradation. The oil industry has cleaned up its operations considerably since the mad rush preceding the 1969 oil lease sale. Still, some operators from time to time cause new damage to the environment. Policing of regulations is urgently needed.

• A close watch on the operations of geophysical company crews doing seismic work for oil companies. These firms operate on small profit margins and consequently cut costs wherever possible. One way of doing this is to leave trash littering lakes and tundra, as in the early days of Slope exploration.

• Preservation of the integrity of the Arctic National Wildlife Range. Established in 1960, this refuge, as an Interior Department publication notes, "represents the only opportunity to preserve an undisturbed portion of Arctic environment large enough to be biologically self-sufficient. It is one of the most magnificent wildlife and wilderness areas in North America. . . Among the wildlife are the grizzly, black and polar bears, caribou, Dall sheep, moose, wolverines and other fur animals, waterfowl and upland nesting birds. Management is directed to maintaining natural conditions. This refuge is expected to yield rich results from studies of biological features of an undisturbed Arctic environment. . . ."

Unfortunately, there are geological structures in the Arctic Wildlife Range that oilmen are particularly interested in because they may be directly related to the oil-bearing structures nearby at Prudhoe Bay. Thus, tremendous pressure is likely to develop to release the Wildlife Range for oil development as well.

11. Prospects

When the state legislature convened at the tiny
capital of Juneau in January, 1970, it was with an
air of optimism and a sense of high purpose. The
discovery of oil under the North Slope constituted a
watershed for the state, promising to transform it
overnight from one of the poorest in the union
to—at least in theory—the richest. Already, plans
had been set in motion to spend the $900 million in
oil lease payments. The Legislative Council, bipar-
tisan interim arm of the legislature, had hired the
Brookings Institution to coordinate a series of semi-
nars designed to explore the needs of the state and
make recommendations on how to allocate the oil
money. Governor Keith H. Miller, meanwhile,
had retained the Stanford Research Institute to do
the same thing for his administration. The leaders

of the House and Senate predicted a session of perhaps 90 days in which legislators would concentrate on issues and avoid partisan politics. Governor Miller told the 60 legislators at a joint session: "Let us work together to do not only what is necessary, but also that which is right. We have come here to rendezvous with history. What we do will not soon be forgotten."

But as the days wore into weeks and the weeks into months, many legislators only wished that what they—and the governor—were doing *could* be forgotten. The session did not run for a mere 90 or 100 days—it dragged on interminably. Partisan politics, as usual, did become an issue. There were crackpot schemes; there was irresponsible handling of state money. It was not until 147 days after convening, in the small hours of June 7, that the session finally ended. The legislators were bone-weary, and optimism had long since evaporated. Indeed, 1970 turned out to be a year of false hopes raised only to be dashed by reality.

Shortly after the legislature convened, Governor Miller submitted a proposed budget of $242 million for fiscal 1970-71—well up from the $154 million for the previous fiscal year. But by the time the legislature was through bolstering the programs in which it was interested—and folding in an unprecedented amount of pork—the final figure was $314 million, an increase of more than 100 percent in a single year.

As the legislature worked on the budget and the

session lengthened, it became clear that the pipeline project was totally stalled. The reasons seemed clear enough: the inability of the pipeline company to provide the kind of information the Interior Department insisted on having before issuing a construction permit, and lawsuits filed by conservation organizations and the native community of Stevens Village, which claimed land the pipeline would cross. Many Alaskans accused the Interior Department of dragging its feet to appease conservationists —or "outside preservationists," as it became increasingly popular to call them. So, late in April, Governor Miller, at state expense, chartered a DC8, loaded it with some 120 Alaskans, and flew them to Washington to lobby key congressmen and the Interior Department for approval of the pipeline project. The congressmen told them it was up to Secretary Hickel and the Interior Department told them the pipeline wasn't going anywhere until the consortium came up with the answers to some rather pressing questions. So the party went home, without the pipeline and little wiser than if they had been reading the hometown newspapers.

By this time it was also clear that the access road north of the Yukon River would not be started either. There were two reasons for this: the lawsuits blocked it and the oil companies weren't interested in spending any of their own money to build a road to nowhere until they were certain they were going to get a pipeline permit. This angered a sizable— and influential—number of businessmen, who had much to gain if work proceeded. This group, centered primarily in Fairbanks, carried considerable weight in the Republican party and it was no secret that its members were making their discontent known to Governor Miller, a Republican himself. In addition, Miller and his advisers apparently had come to the conclusion that economic disaster was in store for the state unless work on the road proceeded. As a result, the governor attempted an end run around the Interior Department and the courts by threatening to invoke an 1866 statute allowing the states to construct roads over public domain lands unreserved for other purposes. There was, however, some question about who would pay for this $120 million project. Miller proposed that the state build the road under the 1866 provision and that the industry repay the state if a pipeline construction permit were received by June 1, 1971. After that, there was the possibility of repayment in part or in full under certain conditions. This proposal was worked out in consultation with the oil industry, and the companies involved favored it because it offered a convenient out if no pipeline construction permit materialized. In fact, under some circumstances, it offered the possibility of a free access road, or one that could be had for considerably less than it had cost the state to build.

This possibility was not lost on the legislature, which made it clear that the chances of the administration's bill passing—at least in the form in which it was proposed—were dim indeed. The legislature

was in no mood for a $120-million giveaway, as
some legislators termed the governor's proposal.
But on the other hand, the lawmakers, who had
been in session for more than four months by that
time and had little to show for it, were operating in
a mood that frequently bordered on hysteria. They
were looking for some grand gesture with which to
conclude their dilatory deliberations. Most of them
wanted to get the pipeline project going if at all
possible and, perhaps more important to some, they
wanted to look good in an election year. So the
legislature rewrote the governor's bill to provide
for state construction of the road with repayment in
full by the oil industry within five years, regardless
of whether a pipeline construction permit was ever
issued. Meanwhile, a determined group of legislators
balked at what appeared to them an unwarranted
concession to the oil industry. Some wanted to see
a slower pace of oil development and thus were
opposed to any state road bill; some had long fa-
vored a higher oil and gas severance tax on the
ground that the state's total take from the oil companies in taxes and production royalties (a combined levy of 16½ percent at that time) was too
low. So, in exchange for passage of the road bill,
this group forced through a new sliding-scale
severance tax based on oil well productivity. It
levied a tax that was only slightly higher on the
marginally profitable Kenai and Cook oil fields,
but guaranteed that the wells the industry was drilling on the North Slope, which were expected to be

highly productive, would be taxed at a rate of about 20 percent when the crude there began to flow through the pipeline.

In these closing days of the legislative session, the oil company lobbyists, who had exercised considerable influence over the lawmakers earlier, lost control of the situation altogether. The oil firms did not want the revamped road bill for the obvious reason that under it they would be required to pay for the road within five years regardless of whether it was of any use to them. And needless to say, they were bitterly opposed to any increase in taxation. But they were powerless to alter the course of events, despite an intense pressure campaign that included political threats against legislators by at least one oil company lobbyist. Many legislators had become hypnotized by the road bill, some even convincing themselves that the industry would go along with it in the end. And the supporters of the severance tax increase were in no mood for backing down. So the oil industry got two bills it didn't want—and a bruising lesson in frontier politics. The legislature passed the road and severance tax bills, the budget and other key bills, then went home. When the industry rejected the legislature's road bill, Governor Miller, in an action that was widely criticized, called a special session to come up with a compromise on which the industry and the lawmakers could agree. It became rapidly apparent, however, that there was no such middle ground and the governor was forced to call off the special session before it ever convened.

Throughout this long, tedious, and frequently disagreeable period, the governor, aided from time to time by Secretary Hickel, various newspaper editorial writers and minor politicians, contributed greatly to a false optimism that the pipeline project would be started in the summer of 1970. When it became clear that this was not going to happen, there were widespread forecasts of economic disaster. Even national publications were taken in by this red herring, and "boom-to-bust" stories were briefly in vogue. There was no depression, however. True, unemployment did reach the highest level in years and a few firms—notably two airlines that had over-extended themselves gambling on rapid development of the Slope—went bankrupt. But these developments must be viewed in the context of what had happened in the previous year in Alaska's narrow-based economy. During the peak months of North Slope activity, several thousand new jobs were created and workers from other areas of the country flooded into the state seeking work at the high wages many of the jobs paid.

The tide of immigrants continued long after all the jobs were taken. The situation, in fact, became so serious that the state hired college students to man information booths in Seattle to discourage the unemployed from coming to Alaska to seek work. So it was the newcomers, arriving in Alaska without jobs, who constituted a large percentage of the unemployed. Despite the high unemployment statistics and a handful of bankruptcies, the economy as a whole experienced a modest expansion. Construction in Anchorage, financial and administrative nerve center for most of the state, was at record levels. Most businessmen—even in Fairbanks, which was hardest hit by the slowdown in the pace of Slope development—reported business was better than ever.

Though preoccupied for most of the session with economic problems, the legislature did demonstrate a dawning awareness of the serious ecological problems oil development brought to the state. The legislature didn't do as much as some conservation-oriented lawmakers had hoped; but it did considerably more than in the past. Bills established three state parks totaling a million acres, the first state parks of any consequence in Alaska; a Pesticide Control Board; an Environmental Quality Control Commission with broad powers to regulate projects, both public and private; amendments to the Water Quality Control Act to remove an exemption for placer mining; and prohibition of offshore lease sales (and therefore any oil drilling) in Bristol Bay. The oil industry strongly opposed the Bristol Bay bill and put heavy pressure on Miller, who vetoed it. And the Environmental Quality Control Commission, created in the closing hours of the session following the failure of a bill which would have established a full cabinet-level Department of Environmental Affairs, was left without a budget.

After such a tumultuous year, marked as it was

by so little clearheaded analysis of the issues, Alaska's future seemed more confused than ever. Not, however, to Dr. Arlon Tussing of the University of Alaska, a young economist and one of the state's most perceptive observers. In a telling speech to the Anchorage chapter of the Alaska Press Club, Tussing pointed out that development of the North Slope was absolutely dependent on settlement of the complex native land claims, in which the state's Eskimos, Indians and Aleuts assert title to most of Alaska by right of aboriginal occupancy. "There has never been the shadow of a chance that pipeline construction could have begun this year," Tussing said. "Nor has there been anything that the governor or the state legislature could do to get an access road built this season. This situation was understood by many state and federal officials, by some members of the legislature, by some staff members of our congressional delegation, by many oil company officials, and by some of the news reporters in Alaska. It is hard to believe that all of our high elected officials and all of our editors and publishers misunderstood the situation, but to my knowledge none of them has ever tried to tell the people of Alaska these blunt truths."

Then Tussing delivered a shocker:

"Personally," he said, "I would not give high odds that the Prudhoe Bay-Valdez route will ever be built. There are the conflicts, the disorganization and the political ineptness among the oil companies themselves. There are engineering problems whose importance Secretary Hickel recently explained very well, and there is the National Environmental Policy Act, whose full implications nobody really comprehends yet. I could speak to you on each of these issues, but I want to concentrate on the stumbling block with which I am most familiar, the stumbling block which is by far the most intractable: the problem of native claims. For settlement of the native claims, specifically a legislative settlement, is an absolute prerequisite for the construction of the pipeline, or an access road, or for any other major industrial or transportation developments on the public lands of Alaska. The relationship of the native claims to the so-called land freeze is a serious issue on which the news media have failed to inform the people of Alaska. Regardless of the wishes of the secretary of the interior, there cannot be and will not be a general lifting of the land freeze until the native claims are resolved. It is true that mineral leasing and land transfers and the granting of rights-of-way and special use permits on the public domain in the state have been suspended on the authority of the secretary of the interior, but this suspension is not something that he can simply turn on or off.

"In truth, there are three land freezes: first. . . . is the public land order of former Secretary [of the Interior] Udall which withdrew all the

public lands of Alaska from most forms of
appropriation until the end of 1970, or until
the claims settlement was effected; the second
land freeze is the refusal of the Bureau of Land
Management to process mineral lease offers or
land transfers in the face of a native protest;
and finally, there is the authority and the obli-
gation of the federal courts, under the Organic
Act of 1884 and the Alaska Statehood Act to
preserve the status quo wherever a native claim
has a shadow of plausibility. . .

"The state of Alaska has gone into court and
before the Congress and held that these provisions [of the Organic and Statehood Acts] have
no force against state selection [of public
domain land up to 103 million acres under the
Statehood Act]. The state's position was rejected by the Ninth Circuit Court of Appeals and
by the United States Supreme Court, which
refused to hear the state's appeal. The courts
have held in effect that a native protest against
state selection—and, by implication, against any
other alienation of the land—must be tried on
its merits . . . One implication of this situation
is that the state cannot speed up pipeline or
road construction by selecting the right-of-way
because the state cannot select land subject to a
native protest, at least until that protest has
been tested in the courts . . . I want to stress
again that the native claims and the land freeze
are just one of several sources of obstruction to

North Slope transport projects, and that the litigation we have seen so far by native groups and by conservation organizations is just the tip of a legal iceberg...

"Where does this leave us? We have a very complicated and interrelated set of legal, economic, environmental and social issues, which cannot be resolved one by one, in a piecemeal way. To put it in political terms, there are five groups which each has an effective veto power over any further big developments with respect to North Slope oil and its transportation to market. The critical forces are the oil industry, the state of Alaska, the federal bureaucracy, the Alaska natives, and the conservation interests. None of these groups is united within itself. But if North Slope oil is to be moved to market, the provisions for its transportation must be generally acceptable to all five, and no solution will be acceptable unless each interest thinks it is gaining more than it loses. Putting together a package which satisfies everybody will take some very creative leadership. This leadership might conceivably come from the governor of Alaska, from the secretary of the interior, from the chairman of the House (Interior and Insular Affairs) Committee, or of the Senate Committee on Interior and Insular Affairs. But so far, with the exception of Senator Jackson, none of these parties has given any public sign of un-

derstanding just how complex the problem is
and how closely related are the issues of natural resource development, environmental protection and justice for Alaska natives. Certainly
no one in authority has made any move to
broker the necessary political trades...

"Finally, Alaskans need to realize that the
necessary political compromises, and the engineering and organizational problems, may yet
take several years to work out. This is true
even if the House of Representatives passes a
native claims bill this year [1970], and even if
Alaska has an enlightened and creative political leadership. Such a delay—four, five or even
six years after the original Prudhoe Bay discovery—should not be a surprise to anybody. And
it need not have been a disaster to anybody.
The oil industry has been naive about the
legal, political, and engineering problems it
faces. It has never carried its own political
weight in hastening the land claims settlement
which is so essential to its own aims in Alaska.
... The state's posture has been one of stubborn
protest and legal confrontation—with the Department of the Interior, with the natives and
with the conservationists. Neither the industry
nor the state government has seen the importance of a package settlement agreeable to the
five interest groups: the industry, the state, the
federal government, the natives and the conservationists..."

Tussing's analysis seems to have struck a responsive chord in the oil industry because not long after it was delivered some oil companies quietly began lobbying for a settlement of the land claims. And there remained the possibility that a final settlement of the claims might have come out of the rump session of Congress following the November elections. If the claims are settled, it will open the way for the lifting of the land freeze. In turn, the state could, if action on the federal level still seemed far off, use its power of land selection under the Statehood Act to take land along the pipeline route. It then would be up to the state—not the federal government—to authorize pipeline construction. There is very little doubt that the state would promptly do so.

Exactly what will happen if the claims are not settled remains unclear. Secretary Hickel, before his ouster from office, was considering a partial lifting of the land freeze to allow the state to select land along the proposed pipeline route. He had said that native interests would be adequately defended by preventing land selections near native villages, which is where the Administration feels most land eventually destined for legal native ownership should be located. Yet if Secretary Rogers C. B. Morton chooses this course the native groups would have recourse to the courts to contest the selection. This would transfer the onus for delaying pipeline construction from such public officials as the interior secretary and the governor to an embattled minori-

ty. There would, no doubt, be tremendous pressure
on the natives to drop any such suit. But if there is
no acceptable land claims settlement in sight, it is
questionable whether such pressure would prevail.
Alaska's natives are becoming increasingly militant
on the claims issue, and this is particularly true of
the Arctic Slope Native Association, which claims
ownership of the entire North Slope.

*   *   *

EDITOR'S NOTE: So the future of oil development
in Alaska remains clouded; and given the complex-
ities it is impossible to guess the outcome. One
thing, however, seems abundantly clear. Never before have conservationists had a better opportunity
to rescue nature from the mindless onslaught of
technology. Nor could the battleground be more
crucial than Alaska, the nation's last, true wilderness. In his analysis of the viscous problem,
economist Arlon Tussing quite correctly points out
that no oil is likely to flow to market from the
North Slope until a package settlement is agreed
upon by the oil companies, the natives, the state
and federal governments and the conservationists.
Such a goal implies, however, that once the necessary compromises are worked out among the interested parties, oil and ice will come together in a
benign mix. In view of the evidence to the contrary
compiled by the author in the preceding pages, this
notion seems hopelessly wishful. Repeatedly, the
testimony indicates that, whatever the safeguards

and however well they are enforced, the widespread production of oil in Alaska will inevitably destroy much of that precious environment. That, not compromise, is the issue.

Having already sunk more than $2 billion into Alaska and not yet realized a penny, the oil companies are not about to pack up their rigs. They are depending, as industry always has, on the politics of expedience, on the traditional American delusion that, as one Alaskan official put it, "This country's so goddamn big that even if industry ran wild we could never wreck it. We can have our cake and eat it, too." If the nation's conservationists have the staying power, they stand a better than even chance of keeping Alaska from repeating the folly of the rest of the nation—from winding up not with cake, but caked in oil.

Afterwords:

The greatest remaining wilderness in North America, and perhaps in the world, is the Brooks Range which stretches some 600 miles across arctic Alaska. When Robert Marshall made his journeys of exploration and enthusiastic enjoyment in the Upper Koyukuk Drainage and across the Arctic Divide in the Central Brooks Range (the Endicott Mountains) during the decade of 1929-1939, there were virtually no signs of man north of the small gold mining communities of Wiseman and Nolan, and some outlying one- or two-man mines on the neighboring Middle Fork of the Koyukuk, and at Big

With the exception of quotations from the writings of Robert Marshall, this chapter is excerpted from George Marshall's introduction to the second edition of *Alaska Wilderness: Exploring the Central Brooks Range* (University of California Press, Berkeley). The Sierra Club is grateful to the UC Press for permission to reprint.

Lake to the east and Wild Lake to the west. The
only exceptions were a few tree stumps in remote
spots along migration routes cut by Eskimos in
years gone by with Stone Age axes.

The great expanse of mountain country with
peaks sculptured by wind and water and ice, high
cirques and hanging glaciers, waterfalls and preci-
pices, steep-sided glacial valleys with untamed rivers,
northland wildlife, and plants ranging from lichens
to sedges to spruce, all added to a wild magnificence
and untrammelled beauty not altered by man since
the dawn of time.

The first violent change, the first major intrusion
of the modern industrial world, occurred in the
early part of 1969. News filtered south that a winter
road had reached the Yukon, that it had crossed the
river on an ice-bridge, that it had reached Bettles
on the Koyukuk, that it was moving up the wild
John River, that it had crossed the Arctic Divide at
Anaktuvuk Pass, that it had gone down the North
Slope to the Sagavanirktok River, that trucks were
crossing the Divide, that the great Range had been
split and its unity with past ages destroyed—
destroyed without a public decision, destroyed without the knowledge of most Americans.

The purpose of this road was to bring equipment
to the site of the great oil strike made in the
summer of 1968 near Prudhoe Bay on the Arctic
Ocean. This road, and proposals for a four-foot oil
pipeline with accompanying year-round road across
the Divide and down the Dietrich River—the

easternmost tributary of the Upper Koyukuk—and
a further proposal for a railway up the North Fork
of the Koyukuk, if carried through, will destroy the
greater part of the unique wilderness Bob Marshall
explored and which he described vividly in his
writings.

"The view from the summit" of Limestack
Mountain on the Arctic Divide, he wrote, "showed
a myriad of wildly thrown together mountains rising from deep valleys, cut up by great clefts and
chasms, their bases resting in green vegetation, then
rising into rocks—stratified at times and chaotically
tumbled at others—culminating in unbroken snow.
. . . The number of mountains was bewildering. I
could pick out Blue Cloud 60 miles to the south,
but from it to the summits far north towards the
Arctic Ocean there was not one among all the hundreds of peaks I could see which to my knowledge
had ever been climbed or mapped.

"I spent more than three bright hours on top of
the continent, looking in every direction over miles
of wilderness in which, aside from my two compan-
ions, I knew there was not another human being.
This knowledge, this sense of independence which
it gave, was second only to the sense of perfect
beauty on all sides."

Climbing to the top of a glacier north of the
Arctic Divide, Bob Marshall observed:

"It seemed to be the end of the earth or the heart
of another earth as we perched on this remnant of a
long-vanished age. Everything we looked on was

unknown to human gaze. The nearest humans were a hundred and fifty-five miles away, and the civilization of which they constitute the very fringe—a civilization remote from nature, artificial, dominated by the exploitation of man by man—seemed unreal and unbelievable. Our present situation seemed also unreal, but it was the unreality of a freshness beyond experience."

Then, exploring an uncharted tributary of the John River, he made another discovery:

"Three miles up the plunging creek we suddenly came upon a magnificent lake. . . . Nothing I had ever seen, Yosemite or the Grand Canyon or Mount McKinley rising from the Susitna, had given me such a sense of immensity as this virgin lake lying in a great cleft in the surface of the earth with mountain slopes and waterfalls tumbling from beyond the limits of visibility. We walked up the right shore among bare rocks intermingled with meadows of bright lichen, while large flocks of ducks bobbed peacefully . . . on the water of the lake, and four loons were singing that rich, wild music which they have added to the beautiful melodies of earth. No sight or sound or smell or feeling remotely hinted of men or their creations. It seemed as though time had dropped away a million years and we were back in a primordial world . . . where only the laws of nature held sway."

Time has indeed dropped away since Bob Marshall experienced the joy of being remote in the Brooks Range. It would be well, then, to summarize the history of the past 14 years or more relating to wildlife, people, wilderness atmosphere, knowledge of the region, and efforts to give it long-range protection.

Estimates differ on what has been happening to wildlife, but it appears that, except for natural cycles, there has been relatively little change except in some localities and for certain species. One wildlife expert writes:

"Wolves were hunted ruthlessly in the 'fifties and 'sixties by a few bounty hunters using aircraft. They often took 150 or more per year apiece. Wolves became very scarce in the Arctic, which I presume means the Upper Koyukuk, although by the early 'sixties populations in forested areas were greater than in the tundra. Restrictions on aerial permits and on hunting by nonresidents seem to have been effective because wolves became more common by 1966-67. More recently they have been hit hard, again by only a handful of people, and populations seem low."

There was a shift in the population of the Upper Koyukuk between 1939 and 1956, and again between the latter year and the present. In 1949 or 1950, 13 Eskimo families moved to Anaktuvuk Pass on the Arctic Divide at the head of the John and Anaktuvuk rivers where they have lived by hunting and trapping. Almost from the start a post office was established and planes landed near the village. The airstrip has been enlarged over the years and in the present village, nearby, the traditional

Eskimo houses have in large measure been replaced
by structures more typical of the "Outside."

With the diminution of gold mining, only about
six or seven people were living around Wiseman
throughout the year in 1956, and the number remained about the same in 1969. There also have
been a few summer visitors and some nonresident
prospectors who have come to do assessment work
on their claims.

The main change in the Upper Koyukuk, other
than at Anaktuvuk Pass, has been the appearance of
some six couples living at different isolated places.
Two do a little mining; four from the Outside
apparently just like the life of the wilderness. During the summer months, there have been increasing
numbers of people coming into the region for re-
creation or hunting.

The major factor, until 1969, in changing the
environment of the Brooks Range Wilderness has
been aircraft. Commercial and military planes fly
over the mountains, and, within the past year, a
great many planes have carried passengers and many
tons of freight to the Prudhoe Bay oil developments. Even more significant for the fate of this
wilderness—other than what the air transportation
to Prudhoe Bay portends—has been the increasing
number of hunters and fishermen, prospectors, and
yes, recreationists who land within the wilderness.

There is a great difference between flying to the
last community at the edge of the wilderness, as
Bob Marshall did, and landing within wilderness.

When Bob and his companion walked with heavy
packs to Grizzly Creek near the Arctic Divide,
where they camped 101 miles from the nearest other human being, they would have been outraged
and their splendid wilderness solitude shattered had
a plane landed with a prospector, a hunter, an
administrator, or a hardware-laden mountaineer.
The environment of their wild camp would have
been disturbed further, although not to the same
degree, had there been sound pollution from a
plane overhead. Eventually, if there is to be any full
wilderness left, it will be necessary to zone areas
where aircraft may and may not land.

There have been two major efforts, since 1956, to
preserve large areas of Brooks Range wilderness.
Secretary of the Interior Fred A. Seaton, following
several years of field studies and educational efforts
by Alaskans, scientists, and conservation organizations, such as The Wilderness Society and the Sierra Club, established the nine-million-acre Arctic
Wildlife Range in the northeastern corner of Alaska. It extends from the Canning River on the west
to the Canadian boundary on the east, and from the
Arctic Ocean some 140 miles south across the
Brooks Range. It is especially noted for its wildlife,
its high peaks, and the extent and variety of its
wilderness.

The second effort grew out of studies made by
the National Park Service of areas of national park
quality. It also grew out of an increasing concern
among a number of Alaskans and conservationists

throughout the nation that reasonably large parts of Alaska be retained in their natural condition because here was where most of the big wilderness of America remained. In December, 1968, Secretary of the Interior Stewart L. Udall proposed the establishment of the Gates of the Arctic National Monument. It was to have two units. The smaller eastern one was to be about half a million acres. It was to include Mount Doonerak and its neighboring dramatic mountain and deep valley country, extend across the Arctic Divide to about Cocked-hat Mountain, and include the upper North Fork of the Koyukuk and its tributaries, the upper Hammond River, and the Gates of the Arctic themselves.

The larger western unit was to be about three and a half million acres. It was to include the upper drainages of the Alatna, Noatak, and Kobuk rivers, Mount Igipak in the Schwatka Mountains and the Arrigetch Peaks west of the Alatna, and Walker Lake. It was to extend in part from a little north of the Arctic Divide to the Arctic Circle. The John River drainage and the western part of the North Fork Drainage between these two units were omitted. Despite some weaknesses, especially making the eastern Mount Doonerak unit considerably smaller than desirable, the national monument would have been splendid. However, although a proclamation to establish the Gates of the Arctic National Monument awaited President Johnson's signature, for some reason he failed to sign it before leaving office in January, 1969.

Later in the year, in the new Congress, Representative John P. Saylor of Pennsylvania, minority leader of the House Committee on Interior and Insular Affairs and staunch conservationist, introduced a bill (HR 11423) to establish a Gates of the Arctic National Park with boundaries and areas of its two units the same as those proposed by Secretary Udall.

If the great wildernesses of the Brooks Range and of the Upper Koyukuk in particular are to be saved, many more individuals and organizations in and out of government must speak up now, and many have done so. One of them is Samuel A. Wright, biologist and former professor of social ecology at a graduate theological seminary. He and his wife spent a winter in an isolated cabin at Big Lake in the eastern Koyukuk Drainage. In his testimony on the proposed trans-Brooks Range pipeline and road at the Interior Department hearings at Fairbanks, August 26, 1969, he warned of the fate of the Brooks Range wilderness unless people speak out. He said:

"We have chosen to live in this last great wilderness, disturbing it as little as possible and becoming a part of its ecology. One reason for this choice was the recognition that at this moment in history this great wilderness is doomed unless voices speak out in its behalf. And, certainly, a voice should come from the wilderness itself."

Forty-one years ago, Robert Marshall gave his

now famous call to action to those who value wilderness. What he proclaimed then, soon after his first journey into the Upper Koyukuk country, applies equally today to the future of the Central Brooks Range and to wilderness in general:

"There is just one hope of repulsing the tyrannical ambition of civilization to conquer every niche on the whole earth. That hope is the organization of spirited people who will fight for the freedom of the wilderness."

—*George Marshall*

In August, 1969, at the Twentieth Alaska Science Conference in Fairbanks, the issue of extracting oil from the North Slope of the Brooks Range received its first full-scale review. At that time I expressed the concern of conservationists about arctic development, commenting that in the latter half of the twentieth century we had not changed certain ideas which were held a century before. We were still regarding our natural resources as short-term economic bonanzas to be grabbed as fast as possible. With our new technology, we could grab more rapidly, more efficiently and far more destructively than we could 100 years before. And we are still in there, grabbing.

The present exploitation of the North Slope illustrates this in three graphic ways.

First, although we recognize that there are other important values in the North Slope, its development has proceeded on the *a priori* assumption that the most important value is the economic value of oil. And so, while we talk about the importance of the arctic wildlife—the fish, the bear, the wolves, the waterfowl, and the caribou, we all know that they are secondary to the oil. While we talk of the rights of the natives of the North Slope, we know that they, too, along with their remarkable culture, are secondary to the oil; and while we talk about the aesthetic and scientific values of the wilderness, we know that the wilderness values have been disregarded and will be lost over a very considerable part of the North Slope.

Our second old-fashioned approach to arctic development has been the way we rushed into it, even as we rushed into the exploitation of the Lower 48 a hundred years ago and after gold in Alaska 70 years ago. Now, the rush is for oil. Despite the fact that the oil has been there for millions of years and isn't about to leave voluntarily, we simply can't wait to get it out. There has been no careful evaluation of the immediate, pressing need for oil—and yet we act as though we were already down to our last barrel. Company has worked against company in feverish haste to find the richest strike. A road was pushed through the Brooks Range in desperate haste to get trucks through to the North Slope, and the trucks lined up behind the bulldozers. (Many of those same trucks, incidentally, were flown back later.) We rushed through the attempts to construct a pipeline, considered by many to be the most ambitious construction job of all time, after an exceptionally brief period of study.

And third, for all our good efforts to do the job right, we have done it wrong and are inflicting brutal damage to the North Slope. The responsible oil companies make every effort to keep the damage to a minimum, but others obviously don't bother. (We are amused by government servants who try to decide what is "necessary damage" and what is "unnecessary damage.")

In August, 1969, at the Department of the Interior hearing on the proposed pipeline in Fairbanks, the Sierra Club opposed the granting of the permit, listing a number of unanswered questions.

1. What will be the effect of burying any part of the pipeline in ice-rich permafrost? Will the heat cause thawing of the soil and ice, producing landslides, erosion and sumps of melted mud? What will happen to a pipe suspended in a river of water mud?

2. Where will the huge quantities of gravel come from to build the haul roads for construction, the access roads and to insulate the pipe itself? What will be the effect of widespread siltation on the spawning grounds of fish in the streams from which gravel will be removed?

3. If the pipeline is routed above ground, how will it be suspended? What will be the effect

of supporting towers on the frozen ground, on the landscape, and how will they affect the migratory patterns of wildlife?

4. What will happen in the earthquake areas? The terminus at Valdez has been the epicenter of huge earthquakes with massive movement of land. The buildings remaining in Old Valdez following the 1964 quake were considered on such dangerous ground that the state of Alaska has burned them. Yet miles of pipeline are presently being stored in this area and the pipe must travel through it when completed. The Copper River Basin through which the pipeline would also run is considered one of the most unstable areas on the North American continent.

5. What about the bilgewater—the dumping of oil-contaminated water into the rich fishing grounds of Prince William Sound through which tankers must pass to and from Valdez?

6. What will be the effect if disaster strikes the supertankers which are supposed to carry the oil from the terminus of Valdez to the refineries at Puget Sound and elsewhere? We know that the damage from comparatively small disasters such as the Torrey Canyon (27,500 tons) has been enormous. What will happen if a 300,000-ton tanker runs aground?

The pipeline company and the oil companies were not able to answer these questions in August, 1969. I see no good evidence that they are able to answer them in January, 1971.

Preservation of the natural scene and the construction of a pipeline are not synonymous despite the good intentions of the men at the top. Nor is a pipeline a garden hose. It is composed of pipe four feet in diameter in 40-foot-long sections. Laying it requires construction of haul and service roads that do even more damage than the line itself. Damage has already been done in many places by the preliminary preparations. Final construction will necessarily involve further disruption. This pipeline is, in fact, an unprecedented experiment. For it to be successful there should be adequate preparation before, not after, the construction has begun. Up until December, 1970, at least, the pipeline companies have in effect said, "Give us a permit to construct this pipeline. We will do the best we can. If we make a mistake, we're very sorry."

Unfortunately, this do-now, plan-later attitude has prevailed throughout the development of Alaska to date. There has been no overall comprehensive land-use planning in Alaska. In addition to the single-use haul road and pipeline which we have been discussing, unrelated plans are being hatched even now for two other transportation corridors through the Brooks Range: one for a railroad to the North Slope and another for a permanent truck and automobile road. These plans have not been coordinated with each other. They apparently involve routes that would invade three separate passes through the Brooks Range.

If, indeed, there must be disruption of this wilderness, there should at the same time be preservation in a natural state of a large part of that wilderness, to be held for all the American people for all time. In August, 1969, we (the Sierra Club) proposed preservation of a large section of the North and South slopes of the Brooks Range, amounting to over 20 million acres. The scenic and wilderness values there are magnificent. Tundra, spruce and aspen forests, the incredibly beautiful rivers, the wildlife—Americans now and in the future should have the right and opportunity to enjoy such extraordinary wilderness features.

As of December, 1970, the moratorium or "freeze" on unreserved federal lands in Alaska was still in effect. Yet a major readjustment of land ownership and land use was imminent. In the Congress of the United States, Senate Bill 1830 (Jackson) for the settlement of all native land claims had passed the Senate and was expected to be an early item for consideration by the 92nd Congress.

In Alaska there are also high quality, unreserved federal lands which should be designated as national parks or as wilderness. The selection of these tracts should not take second place behind presently proposed legislation but should proceed concurrently. Selection should be made now for large national parks to include the Gates of the Arctic in the Brooks Range, Lake Clark Pass on the Alaskan Peninsula and an International Park with Canada, to encompass the St. Elias Range and parts of the Wrangell and Chugach mountains.

An effective federal-state land-use planning commission should be established as soon as possible after settlement of the native claims. It should be an organization through which the federal and state governments can consider and make decisions about long-range impacts on the environment as well as the development of Alaska within the framework of our total national interest. Such a commission could prepare a master land-use and development plan, for Alaska is still a region where good conservation and good development can proceed together.

In the preparations made for construction of the pipeline, Alaskans may feel that their state is so big and so untrammelled that wilderness is endless— even as the pioneers always saw other hills to cross in the Lower 48 only a few decades ago. Today, to a Californian or a New Yorker, Alaska's wilderness is not so big. They have seen their own wilderness shrink and disappear.

The case for wilderness need not be argued entirely on the basis of fundamental human needs. For Alaskans, wilderness can also be a great economic asset. If tapped, the oil will be exhausted, even as gold was, whether it is 50 years from now, sooner or later. The land from which the oil is removed will not again be the same. Protected wilderness, on the other hand, can remain forever as an increasingly attractive resource that will bring hundreds of thousands of people and, with them, millions of dollars to the state of Alaska. This is an infinite resource—perpetual money in the bank.

Such a view was superbly expressed 70 years ago by Henry Gannett, for many years the chief geographer for the U.S. Geological Survey:

". . . Nowhere else on earth is there such abundance and magnificence of mountain, fjord and glacier scenery. For thousands of miles the coast is a continuous panorama. For one Yosemite of California, Alaska has hundreds. . . . Its grandeur is more valuable than the gold or the fish or the timber, for it will never be exhausted. This value, measured by direct returns in money from tourists, will be enormous; measured in health and pleasure, it will be incalculable."

What has been done and planned in Alaska with regard to the removal of oil has been pursued on the basis of three premises which we should seriously question. First, as Americans in the twentieth century, we have assumed that everything on earth belongs to us; that it was put here for our particular use and that we can do with it as we choose. Second, we have assumed that we can treat different pieces of the earth as isolated entities. And third, we have assumed that we are in control.

I suggest we are wrong on all three counts. The earth does not belong to us; we belong to it. We live in a closed system and are, in effect, passengers on a large but limited spaceship. Even as no man is an island, no land is an island. What we do in one area of the planet is felt all over the planet. The lichens of Alaska's North Slope contain strontium 90 from fallout of atomic bombs detonated thousands of miles away. The caribou are ingesting strontium 90, and Alaskans (native and non-native alike) are ingesting caribou meat. The level of strontium 90 is not yet high enough to destroy either species—caribou or man—but it is enough to think about as we continue to test out nuclear weapons.

The bald eagle of southeast Alaska, our national symbol, is listed as an endangered species, the victim of pesticides broadcast on a global scale. We are obviously not in control. Danger signals are flying everywhere: as a species we, too, may already be endangered. If the use of fossil fuels continues to increase at the rate some oil companies project, it may well be that atmospheric changes will ensue to the point that we will destroy ourselves totally.

Short-term economic exploitation is a luxury we can no longer afford. We have to change basic American attitudes and philosophies to bring home this fact. Before it is too late.

—Edgar Wayburn, M.D.
Vice-president
Sierra Club

About the Sierra Club

"Something will have gone out of us as a people if we ever let the remaining wilderness be destroyed; if we permit the last virgin forests to be turned into comic books and plastic cigarette cases; if we drive the few remaining members of the wild species into zoos or to extinction; if we pollute the last clean air, dirty the last clean streams and push our paved roads through the last of the silence, so that never again will Americans be free in their own country from noise, the exhausts, or the stinks of human and automotive waste.

"And so that never again can we have the chance to see ourselves as single, separate, vertical and individual in the world, part of the environment of trees and rocks and soil, brother

to the animals, part of the natural world and
competent enough to belong in it."
                                    —Wallace Stegner

Why the Sierra Club was founded.
Wallace Stegner's words express the same instinct
that caused John Muir to found the Sierra Club in
1892. Muir knew that the American spirit can only
survive in a land that is spacious and unpolluted.

John Muir founded the Sierra Club to enable
more people to explore, enjoy and cherish the wildlands that are their heritage. He felt that man
should come as a visitor to these places (the mountains, river canyons, coasts, deserts and swamps)
to learn, not to leave his mark.

He wanted the Club to rescue these untrammelled
places from those who see them only as wasted
space.

From experience, we know that these places are
only as safe as people, knowing about them, want
them to be. That is why we work to let more people
know about them.

Time has proven that the people the Club takes
to the mountains, rivers and other wild places, become their most determined defenders.

Through them, the Club helped bring the National Park Service and the Forest Service into ex-
istence; played a leading role in the establishment
of such national parks as Kings Canyon, Olympic,
Redwoods, and the North Cascades, was instrumen-
tal in creation of the Wilderness Preservation Sys-

tem and the Wild and Scenic Rivers System; and led the defense of Yosemite and Grand Canyon national parks and Dinosaur National Monument against dams.

The challenges ahead.
While much has been done to ensure that wildlands will not vanish from our lives, too little has actually been saved. Protected areas must now be expanded: we need more national parks, wilderness areas, wild and scenic rivers, natural areas, and wildlife refuges; endangered species must be protected, estuaries safeguarded, scenic shorelines conserved, and open space reserved around our cities.

The environment of the cities now also needs to be made fit for man: we must be more effective in combatting air and water pollution and the prevalence of chemical contaminants, noise, congestion and blight. Most of all, we must control the growth of human numbers so that a balance may be struck between man's works and the remaining natural world. Technology must be challenged to do a better job in managing the part of the planet it has already claimed.

What programs does the Club offer?
The Club offers programs as diverse as the environmental challenges that man faces. Each offers an opportunity to become involved.

You can join in chapter work.

Active chapters with scheduled events exist in nearly
all parts of the country: California, Hawaii, Alaska,
the Northwest, the Southwest, the Rocky Mountains,
the Gulf States, the Great Lakes, New England and
most of the rest of the Atlantic seaboard. Each mem-
ber is assigned to the chapter in which he resides.

Club publications are issued.

To keep you informed, a monthly magazine is sent
to all members; dozens of books published by the
Club are available at a discount to members (send
for a catalogue) ; special newsletters are published.

An outing program is scheduled.

To help you see what needs to be conserved, and
to let you enjoy what has already been conserved,
a varied program is offered:

● Wilderness outings, usually between mid-June
and September; daily costs from $5 up to $40.

● Whitewater trips in wilderness.

● Ski touring and mountaineering.

● Local trips—walk, knapsack or climb.

● Huts and lodges—14 in California, open to all
members (11 have sleeping accommodations).

How to become part of it.

All who feel the need to know more of nature, and
know that this need is basic to man, are invited to

join. Anyone who is at least twelve, anywhere, can join by merely applying. We will sponsor you automatically.

The Sierra Club is expanding in every way: in size, extent and range. It now has 34 chapters in 50 states, with offices and staff in San Francisco, New York, Washington, D. C., Tucson, Seattle, Los Angeles and Alaska.

Wherever nature needs defense, the Sierra Club wants to be on the scene. We welcome all who want to be part of this defense. With new members strengthening its resources the Club can better act on behalf of all that is defenseless, irreplaceable and voiceless in our natural heritage.

Dues for adults are $12 a year; spouses can be members at half that rate. Junior memberships (12 to 21) are $5 a year. An admission fee of $5 is charged to cover processing costs. The fee is waived for students. Those whose generosity allows them to contribute more can become Supporting ($25), Contributing ($50), Life ($250) or Patron ($1,000) members. Application for membership should be made to the Sierra Club, 1050 Mills Tower, San Francisco, California 94104.

—*Phillip Berry,*
President
—*Michael McCloskey,*
Executive Director

Postscript
at press time:

On January 13, 1971, the Interior Department recommended that construction of the Trans-Alaska pipeline proceed. North Slope oil reserves, it claimed, were "essential to the strength, growth and security of the United States." Yet the 196-page statement prepared by Interior listed dozens of adverse effects on the Alaskan environment.

Later that day, the Sierra Club responded: the decision was "outrageous." Said Executive Director Michael McCloskey: "In its study, the administration admits that there will be oil spills, possibly major ones, that there will be pollution, that the permafrost will melt, that the habitat for wildlife will be jeopardized, that wilderness will be destroyed. . . . The administration has chosen to give the oil companies' profits clear priority over protection of the environment. . . . We shall continue to resist development of this ill-conceived project."